Life Writing Series / 2

Life Writing Series

In the **Life Writing Series**, Wilfrid Laurier University Press publishes life writing and new life-writing criticism in order to promote autobiographical accounts, diaries, letters and testimonials written and/or told by women and men whose political, literary or philosophical purposes are central to their lives. **Life Writing** features the accounts of ordinary people, written in English, or translated into English from French or the languages of the First Nations or from any of the languages of immigration to Canada. **Life Writing** will also publish original theoretical investigations about life writing, as long as they are not limited to one author or text.

Priority is given to manuscripts that provide access to those voices that have not traditionally had access to the publication process.

Manuscripts of social, cultural and historical interest that are considered for the series, but are not published, are maintained in the **Life Writing Archive** of Wilfrid Laurier University Library.

Series Editor
Marlene Kadar
Humanities Division, York University

"I want to join your club"
LETTERS FROM RURAL CHILDREN
1900-1920

Norah L. Lewis, Editor

Wilfrid Laurier University Press

This book has been published with the help of a grant in aid of publication from the Canada Council.

> **Canadian Cataloguing in Publication Data**
>
> Main entry under title:
>
> "I want to join your club" : letters from rural children, 1900-1920
>
> (Life writing ; 2)
> Includes bibliographical references.
> ISBN 0-88920-260-5
>
> 1. Rural children – Canada – Correspondence.
> 2. Canada – Rural conditions..   I. Lewis, Norah Lillian, 1935- . II. Series.
>
> HQ792.C313 1996   305.23'0971   C96-930297-5

Copyright © 1996
WILFRID LAURIER UNIVERSITY PRESS
Waterloo, Ontario, Canada   N2L 3C5

Cover design by Leslie Macredie using a photograph from ca. 1913, "Swinging together—the Wadds and Fraser children, Rossland, B.C." (BC Archives [42345]).

Printed in Canada

All rights reserved. No part of this work covered by the copyrights hereon may be reproduced or used in any form or by any means—graphic, electronic, or mechanical—without the prior written permission of the publisher. Any request for photocopying, recording, taping, or reproducing in information storage and retrieval systems of any part of this book shall be directed in writing to the Canadian Reprography Collective, 214 King Street West, Suite 312, Toronto, Ontario M5H 3S6.

*To My Parents—Children of the
Early Twentieth Century*

Contents

Preface *by Neil Sutherland* ix

Acknowledgments xi

Introduction 1

"We Were Nine Days Coming Out":
By Ship, by Train, by Wagon 15

"I Have Two Sisters and a Brother":
Family and Community Life 35

"We Have No School Here": Education and Schooling 57

"I Have a Pony": Children and Their Pets 79

"I Want to Tell You of the Fun We Had Today": Games,
Hobbies, Clubs, and Community Events 101

"I Have Been Trapping This Year": Hunting, Trapping,
and Fishing 127

"My Father Is Both Fisherman and Farmer":
Occupations and Vocations 145

"I Shall Be a Farmer": Life and Work on the
Farm and Ranch 167

"A Story That Is a Little Tragic": Drama, Trauma,
and Childhood Adventures 185

"My Father Has Enlisted": Children and the
First World War 213

"I Worked in a Pulp-Mill": Part of the Work Force 241

Preface

Many historians have shared the common but injudicious assumption that growing up is a universal process, changing little in its essentials from earliest times to the present. In fact, of course, how we grow up is as much a matter of where and when we lived as is any other human process. We know that children's lives, like those of all people, have continuity, change, and sudden disjuctures, and are intimately interwoven into the society in which they are placed.

New generations of historians have put the lie to notions that women, that workers, that slaves, that aboriginal peoples have no history. More recently, they have discovered that childhood also has a history. Norah Lewis surveys some of its already rich literature in her introduction.

Not only does childhood have a history but children have historical voice. In this collection of letters we hear these voices with a freshness and immediacy that belies their age. Children tell us about their families and schools, about the places where they lived, and something of what they felt about their lives. Most of all, they tell us important things about the nature of childhood and youth at a time that seems remote, but is actually so near to us that some who were alive then are still alive now. Two examples:

First, we see that the current sharp divide between children and adolescents was much less evident earlier in the century. While certainly conscious of exactly how old they were, older correspondents display many qualities that we would now expect to find only in those much younger. They take pleasure in what adolescents today would view as childish things. Sixteen-year-old Helen Hussey, who calls herself "Brown Eyes," thinks "it is grand going through the woods" to fetch the cows. Self-described "Country Bumpkin" writes "Here comes a sixteen-year-old bud to join your club." Even youthful members of the armed forces write to what their counterparts today would look upon as a children's club. Were these young men any less able to carry out their duties than their modern counterparts who are forced to undergo bizarre rites of initiation?

Second, many writers reveal how early and unselfconsciously youngsters entered into full- or almost full-time work. Thus it is unremarkable to ten-year-old Wallace Williams that he is not attending school anymore because he is herding 150 cattle and 350 sheep. When she was eleven, "Western Sheep Girl" bought three sheep. Three years later she has fourteen, and sells her wool as a member of the wool growers' association. Fourteen-year-old R. S. Sarty, self-designated as "Mudjekeewis," has the leisure to write because he is on vacation from his job in a pulp mill. Fourteen-year-old Mabel Sears tells us that she is "a stenographer in one of the biggest factories in Orillia, but I do more than typewriting and shorthand as I use the dictaphone most of the time."

Norah Lewis tells us that these letters are not by any means fully representative of childhood at the time. Many children did not write letters. Of those who did, either they didn't describe the grimmest dimensions of their lives or, if they did, newspaper editors chose not to print their letters. Clearly, not all is sweetness and light. Children fall through the ice, get lost in blizzards, are threatened by grass fires, suffer gunshot wounds. They tell us these stories in a laconic fashion, unwilling, and likely unable as well, to articulate their deepest feelings. Thus William Bridge "got shot in the knee . . . I was in hospital at Toronto for ninety-one days, and never saw anyone from my home all that time."

I found eleven-year-old Kenneth Lyon's letter the most moving in the collection. He tells us about his school, his teacher and her car, his hunting prowess, and his agricultural triumphs. One senses that this list goes on and on because he can't bring himself to tell us his most important piece of news. Finally, however, he writes: "I have a brother that enlisted in 1916. He was killed in action on October 30th [two weeks before the Armistice ended the fighting]. He was 25 years old." We sense a grief too deep to articulate. And, even after seventy years, we share it with him.

Long ago, William Blake wrote of a time

> When the voices of children are heard on the green,
> And laughing is heard on the hill.

Norah Lewis has now joined those who have heard the voices and laughter of children of the past. Now, thanks to her, we can hear them too.

Neil Sutherland
University of British Columbia

Acknowledgments

I am grateful to Neil Sutherland and Jean Barman for their helpful suggestions and sage advice, to Linda Hale for her encouragement and to Sharon Olding and Joyce McLean for their close reading of the letters. A most sincere thank you to my husband, Rolland Lewis, for his help and patience with this project and to Sandra Woolfrey for her encouragement and guidance.

This manuscript is the result of research conducted as part of the Canadian Childhood History Project (University of British Columbia), funded by a grant from the Social Sciences and Humanities Research Council of Canada.

Plate 1. Swinging together—the Wadds and Fraser children, Rossland, B.C., ca. 1913 (BC Archives [42345]).

Introduction

Children both make and participate in history. Until recently, however, their role has been largely ignored by historians. Influenced by the social sciences, historians began in the 1960s and 1970s to analyze the social dimensions of the past, and to look at the history of previously neglected groups in society, including children.[1]

Reconstructing historical childhoods can, however, be a difficult process. Historians have had to abandon their perception that child development is a universal process, somehow unaffected by either the time or place in which a child lives. Every society and each class within that society defines for itself the nature, expectations, and duration of childhood. As peoples' lives change through such events as moving to a different area of their own country or to a new country, they modify their child-rearing techniques and their expectations of childhood behaviour to meet the demands of life in new environments or cultural settings. We cannot, therefore, assume that the experiences of children from one geographical area or social class are representative of all children of the same time period.[2]

But historians were also confronted by a second major problem. Children appear to have left few records of their reactions to the experiences or events that shaped their lives. Furthermore, researchers found it difficult to examine historical childhoods through the eyes of children. As a consequence, early studies examined historical childhoods from an adult perspective, beginning with the effects of social policies on the lives of children. Other researchers traced changes in child-rearing practices and examined the demands placed on both parents and children by these changes. But as historians began to examine written records, reports, and biographical and autobiographical materials, and to collect oral histories, they gained insights into children's perspectives on childhood at specific times in specific places. As an increasing number of child-written documents came to light, researchers found that letters and diaries provided both valuable and legitimate views of historical childhoods as seen through the eyes of children. Although children did not generally write until they were seven or eight, and what they wrote was often scrutinized by adults, historians still found the voices of at least some children who were not silent.[3]

In the letters that follow, we hear the clear and authentic voices of real children who lived in rural Canada and Newfoundland (not part of Canada until 1949) between 1900 and 1920. Initially, children wrote to the women's pages, but between 1907 and 1909 sections of the children's pages were specifically set aside for children's letters. Although the children's letters that follow cover a period of less than two decades, when taken as a whole they provide detailed pictures of rural childhoods during that period.

Every week dozens, and over the years thousands, of children wrote to the children's clubs of the four English-language agricultural publications used in this study: the Maple Leaf Club, *Family Herald and Weekly Star* (1896-1968); the Legion of the West, later the Pathfinders Club, *Free Press Prairie Farmer* (1872-1968); the Young Canada Club, *The Farmer's Advocate* (1866-1968); the Beaver Circle, *Grain Growers' Guide* (1908-1963). In 1907, a total of 200,000 readers subscribed to the *Family Herald*, *Free Press* and *The Farmer's Advocate*. By 1917, 250,000 subscribed to the same three papers, and an additional 33,657 received the *Grain Growers' Guide*. The *Family Herald* and *The Farmer's Advocate* were considered national newspapers, but the *Free Press* and *Grain Growers' Guide* focused on western issues. Subscription rates remained unchanged over the twenty-year period at one dollar a year for the *Free Press* and *Family Herald*, and a dollar and a half a year for *The Farmer's Advocate* and the *Grain Growers' Guide*.

The children's pages were a weekly source of stories to read, patterns and instructions of items to construct or sew, riddles to solve, pictures to draw and colour, a club to join, and along the bottom of the page, letters from other children. To join, youngsters wrote a letter to the club. In return, they received membership pins or cards.

Who wrote to the children's pages? Fortunately, many letter writers included their names, ages, and postal addresses. A significant number used pen names, selected because the pen names had some significance for the writers. Letter writers ranged in age from five or six to sixteen years for all four clubs. Young adults from seventeen to twenty years of age continued to write to the ex-members column of the Maple Leaf Club. They were a diverse group in terms of age, ethnic origin, geographical location, and vocational opportunities, and select in that they were literate in English, their parents subscribed to one of the newspapers used in this study, and they were motivated to write to children's newspaper clubs.

Although a few native Indian children wrote letters, most writers were the children of Europeans. Some were youngsters whose family roots were generations deep in their communities. Others were immigrants from Great Britain, the United States, and Europe, or migrants from other regions of Canada.

Whose letters were included and whose letters were not published? As the newspapers were directed to rural readers, most letter writers lived in rural areas. Editors published a limited number of letters from among those that met editorial standards of neatness, penmanship, and content; unfortunately, we do not know the content of thousands of letters that were not published. Editors usually added headings or titles for each letter that reflected the concerns, interests, ethnic origin, or area in which writers lived. Francis Marion Beynon (Dixie Patton), editor of the Young Canada Club, appeared to be the only editor to set topics or themes for letter writers. Other editors encouraged children to tell of those experiences and events that touched and shaped their lives. Conspicuously absent, however, are letters that presented a negative view of rural life or that disparaged or complained of parents, guardians, or teachers. If any children wrote telling of physical, sexual, or psychological abuse or of any kind of neglect, those letters were never published. Revelations of mistreatment or acute poverty did not fit the idyllic rural world that agricultural publications wished to convey.[4] Although the letters presented rural life as ideal, they still provide an exceptional window into rural childhoods in Canada and Newfoundland.

At the time these letters were written, Canada was experiencing an unprecedented period of political growth and rapid economic development. Hundreds of thousands of immigrants poured into Canada seeking adventure, a better life, economic success, or religious or political freedom. Most immigrants headed west to take up farms or ranches in prairie regions or to the rapidly developing urban and industrial areas of Ontario and Quebec. Canada was a nation on the move as expanding rail, road, and boat systems carried passengers across the nation and into the hinterlands, wheat to seaports for shipment to overseas markets, and manufactured goods and raw materials to and from central Canada for domestic and overseas markets. Little wonder Canada's political and economic leaders optimistically touted the twentieth century as "Canada's Century," an optimism shared by both long-time residents and recent immigrants alike.[5] The youngsters' letters indicate they had an awareness of growth and change within their own communities, of past achievements, and of current developments in other areas.

Changes did not occur as rapidly in the Dominion of Newfoundland. Fishing was the basis for settlement of the island, and in 1900 most of the rural population lived in outports around the rocky coasts of Labrador and Newfoundland. As their lives revolved around the fishing industry, most men and older boys fished. A significant number also participated in the annual seal hunt. Women and older girls salted and dried the fish after the catch was landed. Girls also cared for younger siblings and looked after the house, livestock, and garden during the fishing season. Some rural families, however, made their livelihood outside the fishing industry. They hunted and trapped along inland rivers and through interior marshes. Others logged the white pine forests, or worked in either the Belle Island mine or the Corner Brook paper mill. Because of poor soil and the harsh North Atlantic climate, commercial agriculture was limited, although rural families generally supplemented their regular diet of fish with produce from their kitchen gardens. Few vocational choices were open to rural Newfoundland children.[6]

The letters that follow tell us how rural children looked upon the positive dimensions of their economic and social environment in the early years of this century. They shared common experiences of isolation, hard work, few amenities, limited educational opportunities, restricted social life, and heavy responsibilities. Whether long-time residents or recent newcomers, they were proud of their ethnic heritage or regional roots. For most settler children, the future appeared hopeful—they believed their success was assured if they worked hard.

Although those who wrote did not say so, the future of many First Nations children must have seemed bleak and hopeless. Their population had been decimated by disease and their communities adversely affected by alcohol. By 1900, many Indians bands were living on reserves, unable to follow their traditional way of life, and were socially and physically isolated from Canadian society in general and their settler neighbours in particular. Unlike the expanding world of settler children, their world was contracting and becoming more restrictive.[7]

Children were accepted as integral and important participants in both the working life and social activities of country life. To their parents they were the future of the family and their old age security, as well as an essential part of the family work unit. Until youngsters entered the paid work force, their identities were tied to their fathers' or, in some cases, their mothers' occupations. But once they became wage earners their identities were defined by their own occupations as farmers, fishermen, railroad time keepers, mill workers, telegraphers, or soldiers.

The lives of most rural children revolved around work and school. Their days were circumscribed by a round of repetitive chores and their years by a seasonal cycle of tasks, all of which were essential to the family business.[8] Children were a cheap and readily accessible source of labour. Their work, paid and unpaid, both within and outside the home, made significant and sometimes essential contributions to family incomes.[9] By age three or four, rural children were helping about the home and garden. By age thirteen or fourteen, boys were doing the work of men, as fishermen, farmers, hunters, trappers, or working in mills or the woods. At the same age, girls were able to do most tasks about the house and garden, help with milking, tend the poultry, and care for younger children. Pre-teens and teenagers of both sexes regularly hired out as labourers or domestics to help support their families. Nor was it unusual for a teenage girl to assume management of the home and care of siblings when her mother died or suffered chronic illness.[10]

As rural children were less constrained by sexual-cultural divisions of labour than adults, they were often the busiest and most diverse and versatile workers in the community. It was, for example, acceptable for boys to perform tasks generally deemed girl's work, and for girls to perform tasks generally deemed boy's work.[11]

Many children found satisfaction, if not pleasure, in their daily chores and duties. They were anxious to own their own farms or fishing boats or operate their own trap lines. In their letters they proudly listed the skills they had mastered and the work they were performing. It was through their work that children developed a sense of identity, independence, self-worth, and confidence in their own resourcefulness and ability to modify, adapt, and succeed at whatever vocation they chose to follow.[12]

But young rural workers were vulnerable to exploitation, abuse, and neglect by parents, guardians, and employers. A growing body of federal and provincial legislation and child care regulations set controls on working conditions, hours of work, and rates of pay for children employed in factories, mines, and mills.[13] But little or no attention was paid to the working conditions of rural children. With few legal constraints, rural children were often saddled with responsibilities and tasks far beyond their emotional maturity, body size, or physical strength. Furthermore, a persistent myth, fostered by idealistic social reformers, child savers, and the agricultural press, asserted that hard work and clean country air developed strong bodies and healthy minds in even the most neglected, delinquent, and abused of children. Hence, many orphaned, neglected, or delinquent Canadian children and thousands of British immigrant children provided an additional large and readily accessible pool of cheap farm labourers and domestic workers.[14] The childhood years for such youngsters were of short duration, and too many youngsters were left broken in body and spirit and bitter of heart by mistreatment.[15]

Schooling was also an important part of the lives of rural children. By 1900, most parents, including First Nations parents, were concerned that their children acquire at least basic literacy skills. Where and when numbers warranted, parents organized and operated local schools. As school attendance was not yet compulsory in all provinces or in Newfoundland, the actual days children attended varied by the number of days the school was in session, the season of the year, the age and sex of the children, the distance from home to school, road and weather conditions, family attitudes, and whether the children were needed to help at home or to earn money by hiring out.[16] A significant number of children were home-schooled, boarded-away, or enrolled in convents or boarding schools. In some cases, local schools were not yet opened. In other cases, parents wanted their children to attend schools where they would receive religious or ethnic training.[17]

For some children, school was a wonderful experience—a place to learn to read and write as well as a place to learn some arts and crafts. They had an opportunity to play and work with other children and to participate in team games or organized sports. Children made their own open-air ice rinks and baseball diamonds where they played "shinny" hockey and "scrub" baseball. Those who loved school were unhappy when work responsibilities or the lack of high school facilities forced them to withdraw, and thus restricted their vocational choices.

To other children, school was a torture to be endured. They were anxious to pursue their own vocational interests; they saw little value in book learning. For some, their ability to learn was hindered by unrecognized learning disabilities. All too frequently, children suffered overt discrimination because of physical or mental disabilities or because they belonged to particular immigrant groups or social classes. Yet, in spite of the weaknesses and shortcomings of the rural school system, many successful Canadian and Newfoundland men and women were products of the system.[18]

Lack of opportunity, family poverty, or the indifference of parents or guardians also restricted the amount of schooling a child received. School attendance declined sharply after age fifteen, the legal school-leaving age in most areas. Girls were likely to remain in school longer than boys. Parents, particularly mothers, encouraged daughters to become teachers, nurses, stenographers, or telegraphers rather than be trapped in the life of hard work and deprivation they had experienced.[19]

In the eyes of parents, schools existed to teach their children to read, write, and compute. Politicians, educators, and social reformers, on the other hand, saw the school as one of several agencies that could train youngsters to become morally upright, law-abiding, hard-working, self-supporting citizens. In addition, they considered the school to be the most effective agency through which to enculturate and assimilate First Nations children and the rapidly growing multi-ethnic immigrant population into the values and mores of Protestant-British-Canadian society. To speed and ensure the assimilation of First Nations children, many were placed in church-operated residential schools, a process that destroyed family and community ties and created institutionalized children.[20]

Authorities also expected First Nations and immigrant school children to educate their parents in Canadian ways—a process of adult education by second-hand methods. English was the language of instruction in schools. Textbooks, curricula, games and patriotic songs, flag-raising ceremonies, adventure stories, and books all sanctioned and lauded British imperialist values of loyalty, honesty, respect for authority, obedience, and support of Monarch, Empire, and Dominion. The teaching of patriotism and loyalty reached a peak during the First World War. Children, along with everyone else, were bombarded with propaganda that asserted it was the duty of every Canadian and Newfoundlander to support the Motherland in her war against Germany.[21]

Authorities appeared to give no consideration to the stress, frustration, and depression this deliberate process of enculturation and assimilation created for children functioning in a foreign language in an alien culture. Nor did they consider the tensions created within homes and communities when children attempted to change their parents. All too often First Nations and immigrant children were caught between the teaching of the school and the values and attitudes of their traditional cultures. Schools endeavoured to make schoolchildren into model Canadians, while parents struggled to ensure that children maintained their mother tongue and ethnic roots. Undoubtedly, some youngsters lived dual roles as Canadian children at school and ethnic children at home.[22]

Assimilation of immigrant and First Nations children into Canadian society was one problem; keeping rural residents in rural areas was another. In an effort to convince young people that rural life was the best life, courses in agriculture, school gardening, manual training, and nature study became part of the school curriculum. Provincial departments of agriculture, university extension branches, and local agricultural associations sponsored the organization of and provided leadership for a growing number of locally based boys and girls agricultural clubs. Members were encouraged and trained in plant and animal husbandry and home and farm management through demonstrations and practical activities. Undoubtedly, many children enjoyed club work and benefited from the experience, but migration from rural areas continued unabated. Nonetheless, the agricultural club experience was a valuable one. Club members who remained in the countryside were more knowledgeable farmers, orchardists, or gardeners; club members who left were equipped with leadership and organizational skills that stood them in good stead in their future vocations.[23] As vocational choices in rural areas were limited, the hope of more interesting, less strenuous work, a regular pay packet, and a more active social life drew a steady stream of rural young people to the growing urban and industrial centres of Canada and the United States.

Because rural families were often isolated from their neighbours by physical distance, if not by ethnic background or language, rural children were often lonely children. They fulfilled their natural curiosity and their need to learn by exploring the world about them. They observed local flora, fauna, and seasonal change as they explored nearby woods, streams, and prairie spaces on foot, on horseback, or by boat. But rural youngsters were also pragmatists. Young hunters, fishers, and trappers supplemented family larders with wild birds, fish, and game they shot or caught, and they contributed to family incomes from the profits of their traplines.

Their loneliness was further assuaged by the companionship of pet cats, dogs, ponies, or other farm animals that served as companions and playmates, although pets, like children, were expected to contribute to the operation of the family business or the comfort of the family. But neither lack of playmates and manufactured toys nor a constant round of daily chores appeared to inhibit the natural inclination of rural children to play. With few materials and a lot of ingenuity, youngsters made sleds, skis, doll houses, and tree houses. They measured, cut, hammered, and sewed, thereby mastering skills they would use all their lives.

But rural life was not always a perfect life. Youngsters knew the realities of sickness and death among family, friends, and neighbours. Poor diets, especially during the winter months, drafty houses, inadequate clothing, improper sanitation, and lack of knowledge about proper health care left both children and adults vulnerable to a number of infectious and contagious diseases. If available, medical services were sparse and fees and medication expensive, hence untreated or improperly treated illnesses and accidents could result in chronic or permanent disabilities or even death. The serious injury or death of one or both parents left children not only vulnerable to poverty but also to the breakup of their family and the end of their schooling. All too often, orphaned children were distributed to families who needed workers rather than families who wanted children.

Probably no single event touched and shaped the lives of so many children during these years as much as the First World War. In 1914, Canadian and Newfoundland children enthusiastically cheered soldiers off to what was touted to be a short war. Children willingly "did their bit" for the war effort. Underaged boys attempted to enlist, and many were successful. Others directed their efforts to collecting money for the Patriotic Fund, the Belgian Orphan Fund, the Red Cross, the Blue Cross (aid for injured war horses), and for books and materials for injured soldiers and prisoners of war. As members of a growing number of Junior Red Cross branches, they knit mitts, gloves, socks, and balaclavas for soldiers at the front. They willingly sacrificed to the war efforts the few pennies they earned.[24]

As men enlisted in the military, women and children moved to fill positions in factories and offices. As farm labour was in short supply, women and girls helped with haying, seeding, and harvesting. By 1917, the farm labour shortage was so acute that the Canada Food Board organized twenty-five thousand urban boys, aged thirteen to eighteen, to work as Soldiers of the Soil on farms and in orchards and market gardens. They were encouraged to see their enlistment as a selfless patriotic gesture, but once the war was over youngsters and women were the first to be laid off. Their education had been interrupted and many failed to return to complete their schooling. As they had no specific training or work skills, they were probably doomed to work in unskilled, low-paid, dead-end jobs for the remainder of their working lives.[25]

Children were appalled at the terrible cost of war. Weekly lists of those wounded, killed, or missing in action soon included the names of those they knew and loved. They were shocked at the sight of returned soldiers who were scarred and maimed in body and mind. Over the four years of the war, their enthusiasm waned and they longed for peace. Yet two decades later, many of these same children went reluctantly to war.

Many Canadians and Newfoundlanders are proud to trace their family roots to farms, ranches, fishing communities, logging and mining camps, or isolated cabins located somewhere between St. John's and Victoria. Their family lore and community histories are rich with stories of the adventures and experiences of their forefathers and foremothers. Such stories tend to focus on the isolation of the family, the harshness of life, and the vagaries of climate and weather. The stories recount their skills, abilities, and determination to cope, adapt, and overcome the adversities of rural life. But family lore and community histories also include stories of interesting characters, pleasant experiences, and happy events.

As adults, we are not only part of all that we have met, but also we carry the genes of our ancestors. We want to know who we are and to understand, at least in part, the source of our attitudes. Only a small number of letter writers will still be alive, but as many included their names and addresses, their descendents may recognize letters written by their grandparents or great-grandparents. The letters that follow provide readers with a window into the fascinating world of rural childhoods a long time ago.

Notes

1 For a survey of worldwide studies of the history of childhood, see Joseph M. Hawes and N. Ray Hiner, eds., *Children in Historical and Comparative Perspective* (New York: Greenwood, 1990). For a survey of the Canadian studies, see Patricia T. Rooke and R. L. Schnell, "Canada," in ibid., and Neil Sutherland, Jean Barman, and Linda L. Hale, eds., *History of Canadian Childhood and Youth: A Bibliography* (Westport, CN: Greenwood Press, 1993).
2 Elliott West and Paula Petrik, eds., *small worlds: Children and Adolescents in America, 1850-1950* (Lawrence: University Press of Kansas, 1992), 4, and Ludmilla Jordanova, "Children in History: Concepts of Nature and Society," in *Children, Parents and Politics*, ed. Geoffrey Scarre (Cambridge: Cambridge University Press, 1989), 3-24. Jordanova warns historians to avoid the tendency to romanticize traditional values and to judge customs and actions of the past in terms of current values.
3 Johanna Selles-Roney, "A Canadian Girl at Cheltenham: The Diary as an Historical Source," *Historical Studies in Education/Revue d'Histoire de l'education* 13 (Spring 1991): 105-12, and Gwyn Dow and June Factor, *Australian Childhood: An Anthology* (Ringwood: McPhee Gribble, 1991). Dow and Factor used a wide range of sources in their anthology of Australian childhoods from 1755 to 1949.
4 David C. Jones, "'We can't live on air all the time': Country Life and the Prairie Child," in *Studies in Childhood History: A Canadian Perspective*, eds. Patricia Rooke and R. L. Schnell (Calgary: Detselig, 1982), 185-203.
5 Ramsay Cook, "The Triumph and Trials of Materialism 1900-1945," in *The Illustrated History of Canada*, ed. Craig Brown (Toronto: Lester and Orpen Dennys, 1991), 379-94.
6 Frederick Rowe, *A History of Newfoundland and Labrador* (Toronto: McGraw-Hill, 1980), 324-45, and Robert McKinnon, "Farming the Rock: The Evolution of Commercial Agriculture Around St. John's, Newfoundland to 1945," *Acadiensis* 20 (Spring 1991): 32-61.
7 J. R. Miller, *Skyscrapers Hide the Heavens: A Story of Indian-White Relations in Canada* (Toronto: University of Toronto Press, 1989), 5-92.
8 Neil Sutherland, "'I can't remember when I didn't help': The Working Lives of Pioneering Children in Twentieth-Century British Columbia," *Histoire Sociale/Social History* 24 (November 1991): 263-88.
9 John Bullen, "Hidden Workers: Child Labour and the Household Economy in Early Industrial Ontario," *Labour/Le Travail* 18 (Fall 1986): 163-78, and Neil Sutherland, "'We always had things to do': The Paid and Unpaid Work of Anglophone Children Between the 1920s and 1960s," in *Labour/Le Travail* 25 (Spring 1990): 105-41.
10 Hilda Chaulk Murray, *More than Fifty Percent: Woman's Life in a Newfoundland Outport* (St. John's: Breakwater Press, 1979).

11 West and Petrik, *small worlds*, 4-5.
12 Sutherland, "I can't remember when I didn't help," 271-81.
13 Lorna F. Hurl, "Overcoming the Inevitable: Restricting Child Factory Labour in Late Nineteenth-Century Ontario," *Labour/Le Travail* 21 (Spring 1988): 87-121.
14 Joy Parr, *Labouring Children: British Immigrant Children in Canada, 1869-1924* (Montreal: McGill-Queen's University Press, 1980), 82-96, and Patricia Rooke and R. L. Schnell, *Discarding the Asylum: From Child Rescue to the Welfare State in English Canada 1800-1950* (Lanham: University of America Press, 1983), 161, 223.
15 Barry Broadfoot, *The Pioneer Years 1895-1914* (Toronto: Doubleday, 1976).
16 Patrick J. Harrigan, "The Schooling of Boys and Girls in Canada," *Journal of Social History* 23 (Summer 1990): 803-15.
17 Thomas Fleming, "A Century of Concern: B.C.'s Rural Schools—1872-1988," *British Columbia Historical News* 24 (Fall 1991): 12-15, and Malcolm MacLeod, "College in Canada: Educational Links between Newfoundland and the Mainland, 1860-1949," *Newfoundland Quarterly* 80 (Summer 1993): 10-19.
18 John C. Charyk, *Those Bittersweet School Days* (Saskatoon: Western Producer Books, 1977), 2.
19 Harrigan, "The Schooling of Boys and Girls," 803-85, and Murray, *More than Fifty Percent*, 27.
20 Celia Haig-Brown, *Resistance and Renewal: Surviving the Indian Residential School* (Vancouver: Tillicum, 1988), 12-16.
21 Harro Van Brummelen, "Shifting Perspectives: Early British Columbia Textbooks from 1872 to 1925," in *Schools in the West: Essays in Canadian Educational History*, ed. Nancy M. Sheehan, J. Donald Wilson, and David C. Jones (Calgary: Detselig, 1986), 17-37, and Nancy M. Sheehan, "Education, the Society and the Curriculum in Alberta, 1905-1980: An Overview," in ibid., 39-71.
22 Haig-Brown, *Resistance and Renewal*, 15-18, and Manfred Prokop, "Canadianization of Immigrant Children: Role of the Rural Elementary School in Alberta," *Alberta History* 11 (1989): 1-10.
23 Jeffery M. Taylor, "Professionalism, Intellectual Practice and Educational State Structure in Manitoba Agriculture, 1890-1925," *Manitoba History* 18 (Autumn 1989): 36-45.
24 Norah L. Lewis, "'Isn't this a terrible war?': Children's Attitudes to Two World Wars," *Historical Studies in Education/Revue d'histoire de l'education* 7 (Fall 1995): 193-215.
25 Gerry Andrews, "Reminiscences of a 'Soldier of the Soil,'" *Manitoba History* 15 (Spring 1988): 26-30, and Lewis, "'Isn't this a terrible war?'"

Plate 2. Immigrants arriving on the steamer *Lake Champlain* at Quebec, no date (Public Archives of Canada [C-5654]).

Plate 3. Settlers moving from Montana to Alberta, no date (Public Archives of Canada [C-4971]).

"We Were Nine Days Coming Out"

By Ship, by Train, by Wagon

Immigrants poured in from Great Britain, continental Europe, the United States, and Asia. Migrants moved from one region to another and from rural areas to developing industrial centres. Both immigrants and migrants were filled with hope for a better life than the one they left behind.

An Adventurous Voyage

Dear Maple Leaves:

Last time I wrote I gave my name as "A May Leaf," but as my letter was not printed, I wonder if the Editor would mind if I changed it to "Dover Girl."

I would not care to cross the ocean now, it would be a much more dangerous trip that when we came out from England. We were eleven days on the water and eleven on the train.

We went from Dover to Liverpool and sailed from there on the "Lake Champlain." First of all we shifted our cargo in the night, and if it hadn't been that everybody was asleep we should have been sunk because everybody would have rushed to the wrong side to see what was the matter. Then we struck an iceberg in a very dense fog and ripped a hole in the side of the ship under the water line and from that day to the day we landed the pumps had to be kept going. Once or twice there was fourteen feet of water in the hold and the crew was standing by the boats though we didn't know it. They were pretending to paint them, but all the time they were ready to launch them.

Instead of going to Quebec as we should have done we put back and were towed into St. John's harbor and went across Newfoundland by train and on through New Brunswick and Maine, around the northern shore of Lake Superior and through Manitoba and on to Asquith, Saskatchewan. We stayed there a few weeks and then came up to Mervin, to our own land.

Dover Girl

Margaret Scott
West Hazel, Sask.
Family Herald and Weekly Star
August 2, 1915

From Southampton to Quebec

Dear Maple Leaves:

I said in my first letter that I would tell you about my voyage from England, so here goes.

We sailed from Southampton, where I was born, and when we arrived at the docks we went into a large shed where we were all examined. Then we went on board the big steamer "Cameronia," and after a hearty cheer we said farewell to our native land, the whistle blew and the "Cameronia" went out to sea.

We were told the numbers of our berths and after supper we got into them and slept (not so well as we did at home). I was always glad to get on deck. We were all sea sick.

The next day when we went up on deck the waves dashed against the sides of the ship. One wave came and washed a man's hat overboard, and drenched him right through.

The sailors were very jovial and always joking. It was amusing to see the Italians peeling the potatoes for dinner—about six of them in a row. My brother and I played quite a lot with the Italian children.

We sailed on for some days, seeing nothing but angry waves but one night we looked to one side of us and saw little lights on the shore. They were the lights of Newfoundland, and they were all colors. They were a pretty sight—some lights were higher than others as if they were on mountains.

We then turned to the other side and there was Nova Scotia. What a pretty November scene. One could see the wooden houses and the snow-covered ground. It was perfectly grand! One night a little ship came along side the "Cameronia" and a sailor [went] down a rope ladder and boarded the little ship, for mail I think.

One night we dropped anchor for we were caught in a fog—the fog horn blew furiously. We set sail again and signaled to another big ship that was going to England. She asked us if we had seen ice and we answered, "No." It took us fourteen days across the Ocean, and we were glad to set foot on land when we reached Quebec. Then we took a train to Bowmanville where we still live.

My two brothers have answered the call of the Motherland—one is in England and the other in Belleville. I wish some one who likes music would write to me.

        Old Oak of England

Albert Living
Bowmanville, Ont.
Family Herald and Weekly Star
February 16, 1916

A Sea Voyage

I came from the outskirts of Paisley in Scotland one year ago last May, and I am going to tell you of my trip across the Atlantic. I was over eight years old at that time. We boarded the boat named the "Salurnia" at Prince's Docks, Glasgow, on the afternoon of April 18, 1914. There was quite a bunch of relatives to see us off and wish us God speed on our voyage. We felt very sad leaving them all, but the company on the boat made us feel a bit happier. It was alright the first night, but the second day, Sunday, nearly everyone was sick, myself included, but only for a day and then we were alright again. We had a great time on the boat and we saw whales quite near us.

The next Sunday after sailing we sailed through ice all day and well into the next night. Another boat named the "Corsican," also hailing from Glasgow, was stuck in the ice-floes when we came along. Her captain sent a wireless message to our captain (Taylor) for him to say what he thought of it. Our Captain told him he should know all about it for he had been standing by this last six hours, then he added, "But I am going to proceed," which meant he was not afraid of the unusual state of the sea. We were the only real farming class on the boat.

The night before we left the boat there was a gathering of passengers in the music room where we showed what talent we had. Captain Taylor gave me a sixpence with a hole in it for luck, which I will keep as long as I can, and I will never want for siller (sic) as long as I have it. Next day we went to Montreal, then to Winnipeg, and finally to Moosomin our destination, which we were very glad to reach for the train journey was terrible to us children who had never been caged in before.

Helen Lawson Wilson

Grain Growers' Guide
March 22, 1916

A Lonely Member

Dear Editor and Members:

    Last winter I became a member of this charming club and received the club badge which I think is very pretty. I must thank the dear editor for making room for me in such a cosy corner as the Legion of the West, and I do not think I shall ever repent having joined it. I live with my parents and brother on a homestead away in the wilds of northern Alberta. In Edmonton we lived for a while, then we prepared to come out here. We had a team and at last one day we started out to drive eighty miles on the old, well known trail the Klondike, which is very popular on account of its mud holes. We were nine or ten days coming out, but it should only have taken three days, but it rained when we were coming out and made the roads very bad. There are two rivers to cross. One is the Pembina, which is crossed by means of a ferry, and the other is the Paddle, which has a bridge, but this spring it was washed out. Along the Klondike trail may be seen pry poles which have helped some poor person out of a mud hole, and we left two or three behind us. I was 13 on June 25, but did not have a party as there is only one other little girl up here, so you see I get lonesome very often. I suppose nearly all the members are enjoying their holidays, but I have been having my holiday for a year. Well I must close now, for I can almost see the editor's face. Wishing the club success.

                                      Olive I. Johnston

Paddle River, Alta.
Free Press Prairie Farmer
August 19, 1908

From Butte to Southern Alberta

We started for the Great West, Alberta, from Butte City, through the mountains about four o'clock, April 6, 1909. It was perfect summer weather when we left Butte and after driving about ten miles, we struck snow. In crossing the Elk mountains, we were in from four to six feet of snow. Our vehicle was a canvas covered wagon, to which four horses were attached.

Our next experience was going through a large canyon. We went into it about four in the afternoon, not thinking how much earlier it grew dark in the canyon. After going for a short distance we had to camp for the night. We were on a shelf of rock, with a mountain stream running fifty feet below us. The road was so narrow that the horses had to be led one by one past the wagon.

During the night a train came out of a tunnel just across the stream from us and thundered down through the canyon, its head light, in the darkness, looking like a great ball of fire: and as we lay trying to sleep, shell rock kept falling down on our wagon.

Next morning, on starting out we turned a sharp elbow, then went down a very steep incline. We were very anxious to see the boundary line at Sweet Grass. When we arrived there, there were several families wishing to cross the line, but who were having difficulty with their stock. Getting angry, some of them turned back saying, "U.S. is good enough for us."

The line is simply a cement post about six feet high and about two feet square and tapers to a point; something the shape of cement fence post. U.S. is carved on one side and Canada on the other.

We arrived here June 30, 1909, after many interesting experiences, and like Alberta very much.

Margaret Irene Sibbald (12)

Victor, Alta.
Grain Growers' Guide
January 14, 1914

Thru the Crow's Nest Pass

I am going to tell you about a trip west. My father sold our farm out here and went to British Columbia. He took a car [railroad box car] out there with our furniture and four cows, and a mare, whose name was Maud, and about sixty chickens. Two weeks later my mother and my brothers and sisters and I left here to join him out there.

The prairie was a common thing for us to see, but after we struck the Rockies, that is the time we enjoyed ourselves, circling around the mountains. In one place we went in such a circle that we pretty near caught up to the end of the train. In some places we would be travelling on the edge of a mountain with a big river flowing down below us. I was very much scared. One place we saw three pretty jumping deer climbing up a big mountain, alongside of the train. We are back here again as my mother could not stand the climate out there. But B.C. is pretty, with all its spruce and pine and a lot of other pretty trees.

Henry Holmstead (12)

Kristnes P.O., Sask.
Grain Growers' Guide
March 1, 1916

Visited Niagara Falls

Dear Maple Leaves:

I came to Canada from the State of Illinois, a year ago last May. I certainly miss the broad rolling cornfields and the nutting parties.

We used to live on a farm of two hundred acres and we had fifty head of Holstein catle. Now we live on a quarter section, and only have a very few cattle.

We have a yearling colt that I trained to ride. I also have a small horse that I ride.

I like baseball, riding, reading and painting. My favorite authors are L.M. Alcott and L.T. Meade.

I passed the entrance examination last summer and hope to be a teacher some day. While we lived in Illinois we visited Niagara Falls twice. The Falls are certainly a grand sight. One day we went over Goat Island and the Three Sisters Islands. In one place there were many rocks, far out into the water, and we walked from one to another until we were right out into the river. Then we went through the museum and saw many interesting things. I have also been through Lincoln Park, Chicago.

We have a fair at Westlock every fall. This year I won ten dollars in prizes; they were mostly for painting and drawing. I got second prize for the best collection of baking and prizes for some other things.

Bonnie Brierbush

Agnes Myer
Westlock, Alta.
Family Herald and Weekly Star
January 26, 1916

Likes Yukon Best

Dear Pathfinders:

I am coming in for a chat. I have had a long trip since I last wrote. I have seen many different towns and places of interest. I also travelled on the ill-fated ship Sophia on my way from Skagway, Alaska to Prince Rupert, then took Grand Trunk train to South Hazelton, and stage there to Hazelton, which is about one and a half miles. I still prefer the Yukon, my native land, but we all have the advantage of schooling together, which I like very much. My brother and sister and niece will arrive here next week, I expect. I enjoy the letters I receive from members. Just heard from Elgin and Edna today. This is not a very large place owing to a split among the people when Grand Trunk railway was built. [Print unclear.] There are now New, South and Old Hazelton. We live at the latter place. Daddy is situated at a government telegraph office 29 miles out of town, so we only see him occasionally. We will go out there after school ends. He is out in what they call the Kispiox valley. There are several farming in that vicinity; good auto road all the way there.

Hazel Withrow

Hazelton, B.C.
Free Press Prairie Farmer
April 2, 1919

A Wonderful Trip

Dear Pathfinders:

I am going to tell you about a trip to Ontario in the winter time.

Four years ago we thought that we would take a trip to Ontario. We left the place with my uncle. It was near New Year's when we left. There was hardly any snow. We went on the 5 o'clock train, but it was 9 o'clock before it came in. When we got on everybody was getting into their beds. When I woke up I didn't know where I was at first. We soon came into Touchwood Hills. We weren't going over a big high grade, we were going over a big high trestle. Sometimes you'd look down and see some cattle feeding down below. They looked like dots; the houses looked funny.

About 5 o'clock we came into Winnipeg. The electric lights looked nice all in a row. One place in Winnipeg we went over a trestle, and as we were going over this a street car went underneath. The train that we were on was a little late, and the other train was waiting. We just went out of one train into the other, and started off. That night when we went to sleep we were going over the prairie, but the next morning were in woods. We went through a thousand miles of just spruce and jackpine, with little water courses here and there. It was the same all day, and it was pretty lonesome. That night we came to Cochrane. We arrived in Maple Lake, 12 miles from Rosseau, at 8 o'clock. There my uncle met us. We had to drive 13 miles after dark, and it was raining. I don't know much about this part of the trip, because I fell asleep. It was after 1 o'clock before we got home. Everybody was glad to see each other. There was a nice lake beside the town, and a dandy place to skate. There was a good place to coast because there were lots of high hills. Right in the town there was a great big hill, about a quarter of a mile long. The teams used to go up and down this and made it slippery. The police wouldn't let you coast on this because it was too dangerous. You'd be going so fast that you couldn't stop and you might run into a team.

We stayed until March, and then went home. It was just the opposite this time. What we did see this time we didn't see the other time. We got to Winnipeg about 7 o'clock in the morning. When we got off we went down about thirty-five steps and then we went into a room about one hundred and fifty feet square. Many people were going backwards and forwards, some were going to the train, and some were getting off. We stayed in this station all day. In the afternoon my father took us up town, and we had a ride in the street car. Then we went into a picture show. We stayed in there about an hour. Then we went back to the station. My father bought some things for our lunch. The train came at 5 o'clock, and we took it to Landis. There was no one to meet us. Our friend Jacobus took us home. We were glad to see home again.

Roy Grenkie (11)

Landis, Sask.
Free Press Prairie Farmer
March 16, 1916

St John's, Nfld.

Dear Maple Leaves:

Perhaps some of you Leaves who live so far away would like to know something about Newfoundland. As you all know Newfoundland lies at the entrance to the Gulf of St. Lawrence; in other words it is the key to the St. Lawrence. I live in the capital, St John's, and as the city is built on a hill it is sometimes tiresome walking.

From one of the hills at the entrance up the harbour, Signal Hill, a most magnificent view of the surrounding country and the broad rolling Atlantic Ocean may be obtained.

Sometimes when you watch the boats coming in they seem mere specks outlined against the horizon, and they get larger and larger until the whole boat is seen. Some of these are fishing boats for fishing is Newfoundland's chief industry. Every year some 1,300 schooners are off for Labrador to garner in the harvest of the sea, for where else in the world are the waters so teeming with life, and so rich in food for man as in Newfoundland.

The fisherman has a hard life, full of peril with sometimes scanty reward, but they do not complain. They are so merry and they must be very brave to go and face the dangers of the sea in the way they do. Newfoundland fishermen have to work hard for their daily bread, struggling with unknown difficulties that those who have not lived amongst them can know nothing of.

Newfoundland is Britain's oldest colony and is the smallest of those which have the right of self-government. Labrador is under the control of Newfoundland. In the north of Labrador the cliffs are very high and picturesque. Then there in the Grand River; on this river is the Grand Falls. A magnificent cascade three hundred and six feet high or twice as high as Niagara.

I love reading and music. My favorite author is Sir Walter Scott. I would like to correspond with any who care to write. I will answer all letters.

Iphygenia

Pearl Snow
St. John's, Newfoundland
Family Herald and Weekly Star
August 16, 1916

A Russian Boy

Dear Maple Leaves:

This is my first letter to the Maple Leaf Club, but I hope the kind Editor will print it for I wish to tell you about Russia which I think will interest you very much. Russia is the country from which the old folks came, but I was born in the U.S.A. and have heard these things from my father and mother.

In Russia on the Dnieper River near Kiev is where my father lived. He dwelt in a little hut with his father and mother, six brothers and three sisters on a very poor farm which held about five acres of land. They had three cows and had to take very good care of them, that is to herd them for half a day, then drive them back to water and again herd them till evening about a mile and a half from the house. This is the way he lived on the farm for twelve years. Then with sorrow, but with a little hope, he set out, became a sailor and sailed the seas for six years. Then he came to America and lived in the U.S.A. for fifteen years, and then he came to Canada where he has been for six years.

I am fourteen years old and live eight miles from the nearest station which is Loyalist, Alberta. Please send me a membership badge.

Foxy

Family Herald and Weekly Star
July 1, 1914

A Belgian Leaf

Dear Maple Leaves:

    I am writing you a few lines to let you know if I am a german or a english or a french or a belgian. I am a belgian, and now it is war I cannot go back to my county. But when it is going to be finish I think my parents will go back, and I too. I like very much coleman now it is cold. I go to school everyday. I do the work with my mother. I know some little girls who are in the Maple Leaf Club. I like the teacher who teaches me at school, she is very kind to the children. My brother go to school too, he is in the same room as I am. My little sister is only two years old, so she is not going to school.

                                      Lea Panquin

Coleman, Alta.
Family Herald and Weekly Star
April 14, 1915

Although the English is not quite correct, I publish this letter as it is. This is not Lea's only language, so don't you think it is quite good, Leaves. I am glad this little Belgian is safe on our old Tree, but hope that before long she may with safety return to her own country.—Editor.

Four Languages

Dear Maple Leaves:

As I am a Dane and as it is only two years since I came from Denmark I hope that the Leaves will excuse me if my English is not perfect. I know several languages now. I can talk Danish, English, German and a little Swedish and I would love to learn French, too.

I am very fond of reading and some of the best English books I have read are "Little Women," and "The Lamplighter." I am fond of drawing and composing poetry, too.

The boys in school in Denmark had nicknamed me "Either Sex" or "Neither Sex" because I had my hair cut short so that I looked more like a boy than a girl.

I really do hope some of the Leaves, either boys or girls, about my own age 15 (or over) will write to me.

I am very brown. I have brown eyes, brown hair and my complexion is brown, too.

Brownie

Ingeborg A. Dohlmann
Dickson, Alta.
Family Herald and Weekly Star
August 29, 1917

A Little Dutch Leaf

Dear Maple Leaves:

I am a girl, 13 years old, and a proper broncho buster. I can cook and do housework, but I just love to ride.

Some girls prefer city life, but I was born and raised in a big city in Holland and lived there until eight years ago, but I would not trade country life and the fresh air for the smoky city.

When I came to this country I brought a pair of wooden shoes, but they were stolen.

Would some of the girls or boys please write as I can tell them something about Holland.

                                                    Dutch Tulip

Amelia van Koog
Glen Banner, Alta.
Family Herald and Weekly Star
April 3, 1918

Going to Sweden

My parents were born in Sweden and they have been talking about going to see the old folks. They have been saying they are going the same time as the Olympic (sic) come to Berlin. Perhaps the war will spoil it all. It is too bad for the people suffering in the war. Don't all the children in the Young Canada Club feel sorry for the children with their hands cut off? I guess we are all wishing the war to stop—so people do not need to suffer any longer.

When the war is over and the mines are cleared away, I will go and see grandma and grandpa. I will see the midnight sun, the cuckoo bird and the nightingale in the summer; and in the winter I will see the Laplander drive their reindeers, and many other things. I have no sisters or brothers, but I have two kittens and a dog. A neighbor gave me a little white lamb last spring. I taught him to eat out of a spoon, and I named him Johnny. He is big now and has long wool and a bucking machine he really is, but he has no horns.

Harry Vestine (8)

Entwistle, Alta.
Grain Growers' Guide
January 20, 1915

From Sweden to Canada

Dear Maple Leaves:

I live on a homestead about nine miles from Chase, B.C. We came from Sweden about five years ago, but I think I like Canada best. Of course, I would like to take a trip back sometime, but not as long as the war is going on.

Most of the Leaves say that winter is best, but I still think summer is just as good. Still I like sliding and skiing and all winter sports. I love books, like most of the Leaves, and I have read a great many, but I don't think I have read any of Dicken's. I think Alger's are the best. It is over a year ago since I left school and I wish I could get back. When I left I was in the fourth book. I am studying at home now. There is a lot of game here such as deer, rabbits, grouse, etc., also some bears and coyotes. The Indians shoot many deer in the winter, but they also trap lynx and bears, but Mr. Coyote is too sly for traps.

Woodcutter (12)

Herbert Lund
Chase, B.C.
Family Herald and Weekly Star
April 14, 1915

Plate 4. John and Sarah Wray of Nelson Island, near Pender Harbour, B.C., with seven of their eight children (ca. 1902). Both girls and boys became skilled hunters and fishers and, in their turn, provided meat and fish to supplement vegetables and fruit from the family garden (photograph in the collection of Norah Lewis).

Plate 5. The Omer Duval family, undated (Musée du Sherbrooke [P600, S6, PN 7B-3-13] Archives nationale du Québec).

"I Have Two Sisters and a Brother"
Family and Community Life

The rural family was both a biological unit and a work unit with each member making his or her contribution to the family economy. Family ties were important as families were often isolated from neighbours by distance and, in some cases, by culture and language. The death, illness, or desertion of a parent created traumatic and serious effects on family life. In the case of a mother's death, the oldest daughter frequently assumed responsibility for the care of younger siblings. In other instances children were placed with relatives, in foster care, or as domestic workers or farm labourers.

Untitled

Dear Editor and Children's Corner:

I thought I would write and tell the boys and girls about the funny old man who used to live alone near our place. We never knew where he came from, nor whether he had a wife or children, but he always seemed to like children very much. Mother used to send us over to his place every day with some pie or pudding or something nice to eat, and when other children came to play, we always took them over to his place because he never cared how much mud we carried in on our feet, and he would often play with us, and generally he had some candy too.

One day we went over, and he did not answer our knock; and we got frightened and went for father, and he climbed in through a window. He found the old man was dead. He looked very happy and peaceful, and in his hand he held a picture of a very beautiful lady and two lovely children. They buried it with him, because I think he must have loved them.

I like to read the letters from boys and girls and would like it if more would write every week.

One of the Boys

Free Press Prairie Farmer
May 15, 1907

A Little Emigrant

When my grandmother was taken ill, my mother and father was out in Canada. My grandfather was dead. The woman who lived next door went for the doctor. I met her. She said I was not to make a noise when I got home because my grandmother was very ill. At last the good woman came with the doctor. He said that grandmother was to go to bed. This woman was with grandmother until she died. Then she took care of me until my mother came to England for me, and then I came to Canada.

Edith M. Swann (12)

Grain Growers' Guide
May 24, 1916

A Little Traveller

Dear Editor:

This is my first letter to the Legion of the West. We live 25 miles up the Fraser river from Westminster. My mother and my little brother and I came out from England three years ago when my father died. My mother got married again, and she died five months ago. My father was a sea captain and when I was little my mother and I sailed nearly all over the world, So I have done a lot of travelling. I am sending a self-addressed envelope for a button. Your new member

Dorothy Kennedy

Mt. Lehman, B.C.
Free Press Prairie Farmer
August 5, 1908

Wants a Friend

Dear Margaret:

I would like to be a member of your Sunshine Guild. I am in service and should so much like a girl friend. I have no mother. She died when I was a little tot, so that I have never known a mother's love or care. I always feel sorry for members who are ill because health and strength mean so much to us, don't they?

Yours,
M. Q.

Many thanks for your brave letter. It is always so much harder for a girl who has never known a mother's love. Yes, to feel for and help our "Shut ins" is true Sunshine work.

Margaret

Grain Growers' Guide
September 14, 1910

A Christmas Hockey Match

What I consider a real happy Christmas Day is the kind of one we had last year.

On Christmas Eve we placed a Christmas tree in a corner of our house where old Santa Claus could easily see it, then we all went to bed and lay all night long dreaming of the surprise that awaited us on Christmas morning. At last morning came, and we, in our night dresses, ran for our presents, and oh!—but our stockings were loaded. The remainder of the forenoon was spent in eating candies, oranges and nuts.

At dinner time the table was crowded with two large turkeys which we had prepared for the occasion. When we had finished our dinner we told comical stories which we took from the motto "Laugh and grow fat." Just as I was telling one we heard a great whooping and the sound of sleigh-bells and who should drive into the yard but a whole sleighload of boys and girls, and I, not waiting to finish my story, ran out to give them a hearty welcome. They all came in the house where we prepared dinner, for they had driven a long way. After they had eaten dinner we all got up to go to the river in a sleigh, in a very few minutes we were off on our journey, laughing and cheering. It was a clear, cold day, but we did not mind the cold, as the horses went very swiftly.

We soon reached the river where we all put on our skates and several boys went to tie up the horses at a nearby house. Then they all got ready for a game of hockey, which we were all very keen for. It was a very short afternoon, as the game seemed so interesting.

Darkness came before we knew it, but it did not take long to get the horses and sleigh and drive home. On our way back we sang many songs and had a merry time.

When we reached home a warm supper, which satisfied our appetites, was awaiting us. After we had a sufficiency we went to the parlor to play games. The evening was spent very happily indeed.

About eleven o'clock the girls and boys thought they had better get home, so my brother went out to get the horses ready while they dressed themselves up very warmly, for the wind had changed to the north and it was very cold. Soon the sleigh was driven up to the door and the girls and boys got in, wishing everyone "A Happy New Year."

After they had gone it did not take me long to get into my bed which was so nice and cozy that I did not get up till noon the next day.

Hazel McLean

Chatham, Ont.
Family Herald and Weekly Star
December 13, 1911

A Christmas Tree

I will tell you of a Christmas tree that we had. We had a very big tree in the dining-room, and it was loaded to the top. There were a lot of poor children in the town, and so mother and father and we children saved up our money a long time before Christmas, and we bought clothes for them, like mitts and stockings and boots and things that would keep them warm in winter, as well as some toys. We asked them to our home for Christmas evening and we had the things on the tree.

Grandpa acted as Santa Claus. He had a false face on and a big overcoat, and he knocked at the door, and one of us told him to come in. He came in, and when he was walking to the Christmas tree he fell down. He had a sack on his back full of apples and oranges and candies, and when he fell down everything fell out of it. Of course, he did it on purpose.

We had a nice supper, then a few games. After that Santa unloaded the tree and that was the best fun of all. Then father took the children home, and they were happy and so were we; and we thought the reason was because we hadn't been selfish and kept the good things all to ourselves.

Muriel Cooper (9)

Norton, Alta.
Family Herald and Weekly Star
December 13, 1911

Christmas in British Columbia

Here comes a little Leaf from the cold Cariboo, B.C., one hundred and eighty miles from the railroad.

We get our mail twice a week, and all our freight is hauled on big waggons, drawn by eight and ten horses. In the summertime the freight come to Soda Creek and is taken to Fort George by way of the Fraser River on the steamboats which pass by our door, and His Majesty's mail boat the B.X. is the prettiest boat of all; it is all lighted with electricity. But in the wintertime, the mail is drawn on sleighs because the boats cannot run.

I will tell you about my last Christmas, and we had a merry good time. Dear old Santa left us a nice Christmas tree with lots of candy, nuts, toys, fruits and a good Christmas Dinner.

We hung up our stockings, and all he put in them was a piece of candy rolled up in some paper. But I enjoyed the Christmas tree best of all; my little sister when she got up in the morning, she cried and said, "Is this all that Santa's going to bring me?" My little baby brother was angry, too. But didn't they laugh when they saw the tree loaded down with toys.

We went to school all winter in a one-horse sleigh. After Christmas holidays we started to school again. We gave our teacher some presents. We also had a concert, and we enjoyed it very much.

We had one Christmas in Medicine Hat before we came to British Columbia. Santa came around in the streets and gave us each a ticket, and said we should go around to the store and get candy. He went around the streets in a waggon. And all the children in the town were following him. He was throwing them apples all the time. We had a concert in the church and the schoolhouse; we all received some presents.

We had a fine time at our Christmas, and I think that is a very nice way to spend Christmas. I know I enjoyed it.

I have a doll that I got on Christmas when I was four days old, and I have it yet. I am a little Christmas girl, will be thirteen years old on the 21st of December. I hope all the Leaves will send me a post-card shower.

I will close, wishing one and all a merry Christmas and prosperous New Year.

Julia Roberts (13)

Soda Creek, B.C.
Family Herald and Weekly Star
December 13, 1911

A Useful Leaf

Dear Maple Leaves:

Here is a new Leaf asking to join your Club. I live in a village on Cape Sable Island. I am nine years old, and I am in the sixth grade at school. I made the highest average in the school on grading examinations this year.

The only pet I have is a big cat named Dick. I have four brothers but no sisters, so I often help Mamma about the house, washing dishes, etc., and once when she was sick I made a cake. I would like to correspond with some little boy about my own age. As my letter is getting long, I will close by signing myself.

Fisherman's Son

G. Allen Nickerson
Stoney Island, N.S.
Family Herald and Weekly Star
August 12, 1914

Can Cook And Sew

Dear Maple Leaves:

I am thirteen years old, and have been crippled since I was six years old when I was taken sick with hip trouble.

I can not walk without a cane, one of my feet is about four and a half inches shorter than the other.

I only went to school for about two years, and I am in grade four now, but as my mother is sick I cannot go.

I have a brother and a little sister; her name is Margaret.

My father owns a mill and he is a miller. I can sew, cook, and knit. My favorite pets are cats and a dog named Fanny.

I would like to correspond with Mayflower, Moose Jaw, Sask.

Une Bonne Fille

Christine Smith
Grand River, N.S.
Family Herald and Weekly Star
September 13, 1916

Adventures

Dear Maple Leaves:

Here comes another green leaf. I live in Windsor and like it very much, but I like the country better as it is healthier.

My father is dead, and I have no brothers or sisters. I am twelve years old, and my mother is a school teacher. She has taught for nearly twenty years, and has taken this paper for as long as she can remember. We both think it is the best, because it has the finest war photographs, and the best stories of all kinds, and ever so many other things we can't do without it.

I have had lots of adventures and if I get any correspondents I will tell them some. Here is one:

I fell from a gable into a ditch and nearly broke my neck when I was four. Another time I fell off a black horse which had only one eye into a patch of "Canuck" thistles, and nearly broke my neck again. Oh yes! I may have more adventures.

Evergreen 1

Fred Inglis
Windsor, Ont.
Family Herald and Weekly Star
March 22, 1916

A Little Housekeeper

Dear Maple Leaves:

As spring is here I see many new leaves budding on your beautiful maple tree. I am a girl of fifteen years old. My mother is dead and I keep house for my father and four younger brothers and sisters.

My oldest brother is a soldier in England. He belongs to the 185th Battalion Highlanders. I would like correspondents from England and Scotland and Ireland.

Esther McCready

McCreadyville, B.C.
Family Herald and Weekly Star
July 4, 1917

A Brave Little Mother

Dear Maple Leaves:

My mother takes the Family Herald and we like it so much.

I do not go to school, as the school is too far away and the roads are bad. I have three brothers and three sisters.

I am housekeeper, as my mother works in town eight miles away and only comes home Saturday night, as she has to walk. I have a little brother three months old to take care of besides looking after the other children and the work.

I can sew and knit. I am eleven years old. I can milk, too, and I do nearly all the cooking.

Northern Rose

Family Herald and Weekly Star
July 11, 1917

An Event of the Twenty-Second

I am going to tell you a true story of what happened the twenty-second of July in the year 1915. We children went to the neighbors' in the morning and father said that if we saw a flag flying we would know that the stork had brought us a baby. We were playing and never thought of the flag, when we just happened to look back at our place and we saw the flag was up. Then we tried to guess if it was a baby boy or girl. We had our supper with the neighbor and when it was over she drove us home.

When we got home the nurse was at the door to meet us with the baby. She let us hold the baby and the first thing that I said was it a boy or girl and she said that it was a baby girl. I was very glad to hear that it was a baby girl, but my brother was sorry, because he wanted a baby brother. He would not sell her now and we think that she is a darling. She is now six months old and has two teeth. I would like to be a member of your club and receive a pin.

Margaret A. Burke (9)

Delia, Alta.
Grain Growers' Guide
May 24, 1916

A New Baby Brother

Dear Maple Leaves:

    We go hunting gophers everyday. I save the tails and papa gives me two cents a piece. I have seven nice dolls and a doll buggy and other pretty things. When mamma went to the States she brought a nice baby brother—and he is cute. I would like to correspond with Topsy.

                                Snowball Elizabeth

Reklaw, Sask.
Family Herald and Weekly Star
May 8, 1918

Going Back to School

Dear Maple Leaves:

I am a girl of ten years. I have three sisters and two brothers, but I'm the oldest.

Father has been dead one year now and I am home with mother trying to help her all I can. Seeing we have no one to earn for us, we must try and do all we can, by spinning and knitting.

I have been making use of my holidays in helping mother most all the time, sometimes going for a row. I have one uncle enlisted as a soldier to fight the foe.

In winter we have a lot of fun skating and riding on the ice with dogs.

I would like any Leaves of my own age to write to me.

Long Heel

Annie Warren
Bering Neck, Ship Island
Family Herald and Weekly Star
October 22, 1918

An Orphan

Dear Pathfinders:

This is my first letter to your interesting club. I have thought of writing for some time, but something always stopped me.

I have no brothers or sisters and no mother. Mamma died on the 16th of December. I was sick when she died and was carried out to see her. She died in Denver, Colorado. In February I came to Regina. I stayed with my grandmother until papa came down from Denver in the car, with my uncle. I went to school in Regina until June 7. Then I went in the country visiting my friends. Then I came to Riverhurst to stay with my aunt all winter. I am going to school here; it begins on Monday.

I would like any girls my age (10) to write. I will answer all letters. Wishing the club every success.

Violet R. Pederson (10)

Riverhurst, Sask.
Free Press Prairie Farmer
August 25, 1920

Plate 6. A country schoolhouse near Moose Jaw, Sask., ca. 1902 (Public Archives of Canada [C-14452]).

Plate 7. Children riding to school in the Virden Consolidated School Van, 1920 (Public Archives of Canada [PA-48671]).

Plate 8. Sewing class, grades seven and eight, Sir James Douglas School, Victoria, B.C., ca. 1912 (BC Archives [B-03422]).

Plate 9. Jardin scolaire, St.-Casimir, J. Charles Magnan, 1915 (Musée du Sherbrooke [N78-11-16] Archives nationale du Québec).

Plate 10. A gathering of rural schoolchildren, probably for an annual sports day, Virden, Man., 1920 (Public Archives of Canada [PA-48670]).

"We Have No School Here"
Education and Schooling

The school was the heart of the rural community. It served as learning centre, sports centre, and social centre. There children were taught to read, write, compute, to sing patriotic songs, and to honour king, country, and Anglo-Canadian values. They were also taught practical skills of sewing, manual training, and gardening. They learned to work and play with other children. Not all children, however, had the opportunity to attend school, and not all children attended school on a regular basis. All too frequently children left school at an early age to help about home or to join the work force.

From the Far Yukon

Dear Maple Leaves:

Have you room for another Leaf upon your thrifty tree? I became a member about a year ago. I have written one letter before, which I was sorry not to see in print.

I live on a farm four miles from Dawson, across the Yukon River. I came here eight years ago with my mother to live with my father. I have had very little chance to go school while I have been here as four miles is a good way to walk to school in the cold winter. I go to the Catholic School now, and like it very much. The sisters are as a rule very patient. I tell you, if I were they I would get mighty cross sometimes, for we get into all kinds of mischief and talk to "beat the band." At recess we play "Run, sheep, run" "Fox and Goose" "Leap Frog and many other games.

This winter has been good skating on the Klondike River. I went out four or five times and always had a good time with the exception of one generous bump on my knee when I started in.

I know only three other members besides myself in this country. Mary Bird, John McClarion and John Lawrence, at Stewart River, which is seventy miles from Dawson.

If there are any of the Leaves interested in composing poetry, I would like to hear from them.

Ivy, I would like to correspond with you if you would please send your address.

I am very fond of reading and have read a good many books. I wonder how many of the Leaves read "Kilmeny of the Orchard." I thought it a very sweet story. I enjoyed the other stories "Anne of Green Gables," and "Anne of Avonlea" very much.

I noticed Anne, Gilbert and Diana seem to be friends. Well, Gilbert, if you are as patient as our story Gilbert you will win the day. Patience makes the man, so go ahead.

Hoping to see this letter in print, I must close, so good-bye Dear Leaves, until I come again.

Repunzel

Carol M. Stevens
Dawson City, Y.T.
Family Herald and Weekly Star
June 28, 1911

Lives on a Small Island

Dear Maple Leaves:

This is my first letter to your club. My sister wrote and received a badge, I would like to get one too, the little pin is very pretty.

I live on a small island; I cannot go to school, but I teach my brother and four sisters; my eldest brother is away teaching. All the water is frozen now, and we can walk to the mainland.

I like football, riding, and all kinds of sport. I go boating in summer. Birds are very plentiful around the island and there are all kinds of fish too. There are plenty of berries and wild flowers growing here.

It is very nice when spring comes and the birds build their nests.

I go ashore in summer time to the mainland, but in winter we are surrounded by ice. I would like to be a school teacher.

A Lover of Flowers

Eunice Butler (13)
Puffin Island, Greenspond
Bonavista Bay, Nfld.
Family Herald and Weekly Star
March 20, 1916

Rowing to School. Seems Like Holland

Dear Editor:

I enjoy reading the Pathfinders page.

I like winter best of all, because of the skating and sliding. As we live near a lake it gives a good chance for skating. In the summer we row to school and in the winter we walk across the ice. I am in grade five.

Some of the girls in Keewatin have made up a little club and about four or five months ago held a tea for the Red Cross. We made $38 dollars and gave it to the Red Cross. I would like a girl of my own age to write to me.

Signe Hansen (11)

Keewatin, Ont.
Free Press Prairie Farmer
January 2, 1918

At Indian School

Dear Pathfinders:

This is my first letter to your most interesting club. I go to school every day. There are only ten white children in the school, the rest are Indians. The Indian children board at the school, but the white children don't. I am in grade four. We do not do any lessons now, as we are practicing for a concert on the 29th of June. I will close now, wishing the club every success.

Marjorie Pinsent (10)

Onion Lake, Sask.
Free Press Prairie Farmer
July 24, 1920

45 Miles from Railroad

Dear Pathfinders:

I have been thinking of writing to the club for some time and am at it at last. I am in the sixth grade but expect to get into the seventh before school closes. School started April 2, and closes November 30. I have not missed a day since I started and have only been late three or four times. We have a mile and a half to go and drive with an Indian pony. Our school is called "Table Butte." It is named after a butte near the edge of the district, which is called Table Butte because it is flat on top like a table. Our school is very pretty and will seat thirty pupils. There are only ten going now as the rest have too far to come when it is so cold. In the summer we had an average of twenty for two months.

We live eight miles from the post office. It used to be nearer but it was moved. It is called "Lonesome Butte" because near where it was the first time, there was "Lonesome Butte" which it is named after. "Lonesome Butte" is so called because there are no hills within a mile of it and from a distance it looks very lonesome.

We live forty-five miles from a railway. I have not seen a railway train since we came out here, which is three and a half years this fall.

I have a calf that is called Susie. She is two and a half years old this fall. Her foot is sore just now, but I hope it will soon be well again. She had a calf in the spring, but it died.

At school we always play "New Orleans," "Redman," "Tag," and "Police." In the summer we played baseball. The side I was on always won. It is too cold to play it now. Next time I write I hope to send a story.

Ethel Root

Lonesome Butte, Sask.
Free Press Prairie Farmer
January 2, 1918

Why I Like School

I like to go to school I like to read and spell. I like to paint with water colours. I like to play with plasticene. If I get done with my lesson before recess time the teacher gives me the plasticene to play with. Sometimes the teacher gives me a picture book to look at.

I like to play games with the other children at recess and at noon hour. Sometimes we play baseball. We also play hide-and-go-seek, dropping the handkerchief, ante-I-over, kick-the-picket and many other games. I like to play school. There are about twenty in our school so we can play games together real well.

Bertha Newton (9)
Dalemead, Alta.
Grain Growers' Guide
September 27, 1916

Likes to Study

Dear Pathfinders:

    I have read the letters in the Free Press Prairie Farmer and find them to be quite interesting. So I will try to write one also. I wish to become a member of the Pathfinders' club, and am sending the coupon to you. I am going to school and enjoy it very much. The best thing I like to do is to study. I am in grade 8 now, and have to pass the examinations for this year. We have to study hard in school now. We have several subjects, and they are as follows: Geography, English and Canadian history, grammar, civics, hygiene, elementary science, agriculture, geometry, bookkeeping, etc. I like to study all these subjects. Now that the snow is melted again I have to stay home and help on the farm. I like to do this also.

                                              Peter S. Thiessen (13)

Box 74, Herbert, Sask.
Free Press Prairie Farmer
April 21, 1920

A Domestic Science Room

Dear Maple Leaves:

I wonder how many of you have a Domestic Science room at school. We have; it is large and well-lighted. It contains two large enamel sinks with hot and cold water attached, a refrigerator, a large cupboard with glass doors, inside of which dishes are kept, a large kitchen cabinet for groceries, a gas range for baking and boiling, chairs and sixteen kitchen cabinets without high tops. Each cabinet seats two pupils. Each pupil has her own set of utensils composed of two mixing bowls, a sieve, a measuring cup, a tray, an egg beater, a wooden spoon, a tablespoon, a knife and fork, two teaspoons, a granite and porcelain mug, a sauce dish, and a plate. The cupboard is equipped for dish washing. What pleasure! Two of our teachers left school in February for the front. Wasn't it noble of them?

                                      Canadian Lass

Nellie M. Harrison
815 Queen Street, Chatham, Ont.
Family Herald and Weekly Star
April 14, 1915

School Inspector Visit

Dear Maple Leaves:

We had the School Inspector visit a while ago. He gave us a few examples in arithmetic also in grammar. We read for him and answered all questions he gave us, then he gave us a holiday. I wish the inspectors would come every week and give us a holiday.

Would any of the Leaves send me the words to the song, "Oh Canada"? Would some of the Leaves please write to
Pitch-a-Paw

Cleophus White
Shanlon Cove, St George's, Nfld.
Family Herald and Weekly Star
August 22, 1917

A Remarkable Teacher

Two years ago we had a teacher who was very kind. Her name was Mrs. Hardy. She had four children of her own to take care of and twenty children to teach. She lived in a little shack beside the school. Every holiday we had she would make all kinds of candy and good stuff and invite all the children to dinner and in the afternoon we had a great time. On Sundays in the forenoon she would walk two miles to church and take the children with her. In the afternoon we would go over to her place and she would teach Sunday school. When she heard anyone was sick she would go and do everything she could for them. On Hallowe'en she had everything fixed up for a party for the children. The night before Hallowe'en she took very sick. At eleven o'clock she sent one of her neighbors over for my mother. She was very sick when my mother got there. She stayed at home for a week then her brother and sister came out here and took her to a hospital. About two days afterwards she died. We were very sorry. It was not because we lost our party, but it was because we lost a good teacher.

Ruth Nelson (9)

Palmer, Sask.
Grain Growers' Guide
March 22, 1916

Will Be a True Teacher

My idea of a happy life is to be a good teacher. I think to be a good teacher is the greatest calling anyone can have.

Some teachers just seem to be teaching for the sake of a high salary and an easy life.

I do not think a teacher's life is a very easy life if the teacher does his or her own duty. I would not want my pupils to be afraid of me, or to expect that if they do not do certain things in a given time they will be kept in at recess or after four.

I would not want my pupils to be afraid of asking for a little help over some small matter (which perhaps they ought to know, but have forgotten) for fear of being told, "You ought to be ashamed of yourself for not knowing that; why So-and-So could tell you that."

This will silence the enquirer and he will plod along by himself. Consequently he wastes time, gets behind with his lessons and when his class is called he is probably made fun of by the others for not knowing his lesson. Perhaps the teacher tells him to stay in at recess or after four. The youngster becomes discouraged and thinks his teacher does not care whether he learns or not. He falls behind his class and at last finds himself alone, with his class ahead of him.

If the teacher had given a little aid, the pupil would have known his lesson and would have looked upon his teacher as someone who would help him and sympathize with him.

The teacher who is kind and sympathetic, ready to suggest a game and take part in it, will be liked by his or her pupils. The teacher holds in his hand the future of his pupils and he can mould them as he will. He can influence them either for good or for evil, just like the piece of hot iron in the blacksmith's hands he can do with it what he will.

It must be a pleasure to those who really love to do so to impart knowledge to eager little minds and make learning a pleasure, and not a toil.

As boys and girls are, so will the men and women be. The boys and girls of today will be the men and women of tomorrow. They will make the laws, govern the country and help the world to prosper. They will be the lawyers, preachers, teachers, nurses, doctors and many other things.

If they are not properly trained they will not be fitted for the work that awaits them and the teacher can do a great deal towards making them fit. If ever I am a teacher I will try and train the boys and girls to be good men and women who will leave the world better than they found it.

Betsy A. H. Thompson (13)

Grain Growers' Guide
June 23, 1915

Santa Claus

For a long time we practiced, first songs and dialogues, and some took home recitations. Everybody was singing and acting in those days before Santa came. We looked forward to the entertainment to come and for a look at Santa's red face and white whiskers. We had a long program, but at last we got ready and the happy night came. After about an hour and a half we heard Santa's bells in the distance. He came in a motor car with the reindeer's bells on the back of the car, so that every time he turned a corner quick or hit a bump they would jingle, and so that is the way we heard him coming. When he got to the school house he said that he had two big packs on his back. He said that he had come from Edmonton tonight, and his car had run into the ditch three times. It had gone into a snowdrift and had stopped two or three times. Then he was so fat I doubt if he could run it very well. He began to open the pack, which he had brought with him, and take things off the tree. When he got half thru we began to step on his toes and punch him. He got right out and chased some of the children and spanked them well when he caught them. After a general up-roaring time and all the candy bags were handed around Santa went around and threw apples at everyone. Then he said goodbye and left us all hoping to see him next year, at the next entertainment.

Kathleen E. Ramsforth (9)

Lacombe, Alta.
Grain Growers' Guide
March 1, 1916

For some reason I like this letter very much, don't you, little people? D.P.

Our School Fair

(First Prize Letter)

The Kelwood school fair is held annually about the first of October, in connection with that of the Kelwood agricultural society, and I might say it is looked forward to by the majority of boys and girls of our school as the event of the year. This fair has been in operation for several years, but not until 1914 had it assumed any large proportions. Before that time the prizes were enumerated as one section of the agricultural prize list, but now they have a separate prize list printed purposefully for the school.

The prize lists are printed early in the spring and sent out to separate families as soon as possible. It is interesting to look over the list, and single out the items for which one might compete, and figure up the amount first prize in each case would win. Quite a bank account might be started in anticipation or imagination, but realization is another thing.

The prizes are numerous and of good value, averaging perhaps sixty cents for first and forty for second. Special prizes are also donated by private persons, and these of course are greater value, averaging from two to five dollars. In 1914 a special prize of ten dollars was offered for the best map of the municipality of Rosedale. The nature of the competitions vary for the different grades. For example, grades one and two are tested in raffia and plasticine work, wool weaving and writing, while the higher grades are tested in writing, different kinds of drawing and essay writing. Also other prizes are given for garden and domestic products.

The time of preparation before the fair is always interesting. Everyone does his work well, and as there is always plenty of competition, it often takes no mean effort to excel the others. The exhibits are placed in the hall by teachers and pupils and judged the night previous to the fair day, and when the hall is opened the next day there is always a rush of boys and girls to see who are the prize winners. Due attention is given to the school work by the adults also. In 1915 special attention was given to the bread made by girls under fourteen years of age. It was really excellent. The work done by the little tots is always very pretty. In 1914 a little girl in grade two showed a miniature wool hammock. It looked real cute and was done very neatly. I think a school fair is very beneficial to the boys and girls, as it has the effect of making them more interested in their work. Our fair has been very successful, as parents, pupils and teachers all seem to take an interest in it.

Elsie Hamilton (17)

Kelwood, Man.
Grain Growers' Guide
March 29, 1916

Studies Evolution

Dear Pathfinders:

Some time ago one of the Pathfinders suggested that more interesting subjects should appear in the Pathfinders' Page. I am also of his opinion.

My father gave me last summer Dennis Hird's two books of "Evolution." It is a scientific work and very interesting.

It explains how the world and the millions of other planets have been formed from the infinite gas through an evolutionary process.

It also explains the origin of the species. It shows that the first form of life which came into existence on our planet is found in the seaweed; it is called the amoeba.

I strongly recommend this work to Pathfinders—it is certainly an eye-opener.

Rene Adams (12)

Crane River, Man.
Family Herald and Weekly Star
December 1, 1920

A School Picnic

Dear Maple Leaves:

How many of you saw or heard the gas well at Oil Springs? We could hear it for miles around. Its roar sounded like that of a train. But I did not have the pleasure of seeing it. Some of the neighbors who went to see it had to fill their ears with batting. It would have been a fine sight to see the gas shooting up into the air. One man had his dog in his buggy with him while on the grounds, and the dog was overcome with gas. But after awhile the dog came around and was none the worse for his accident.

I suppose some of the Leaves were at the school pic-nic which was held in Trott's woods in Oil City. I certainly enjoyed myself. A neighbor of ours took a load of children. The wagon was decorated with Maple Leaves with the Union Jack and the school banner flying above. Our school was to represent Britain. The boys were dressed as soldiers. Their coats were red with brass buttons, black collars and white belts. Their overalls were also long and black with a red stripe down each side. The girls were dressed in white with red, white and blue sashes, each child wore a white crown with their hair hanging and carried a flag.

Our school was successful in securing the first prize for the best costume. It was grand to see all the children marching with the band leading them. They also had songs, speeches, and music. For amusement they had races, basket and baseball, and the merry-go-round.

I will now close, hoping I have not tired the Leaves too much. If any of the members or ex-members care to write to me I will answer all favors. Wishing the Leaves and Editor success, I remain

Your sincere friend,
Mabel Aileen Core

Petrolia, Ont.
Family Herald and Weekly Star
September 2, 1914

Enjoyed Picnic

Dear Pathfinders:

Oh! ain't it a grand and glorious feeling? I'll say it is. I have just received word that I have passed my entrance examination and I certainly am glad. The mathematics were very hard and only four from near here passed. But I was one of the lucky four. After holidays I intend to take up high school work. On the first of July four schools from around here had a union picnic. At the beginning there was a calathumplan parade from the town school to the picnic grounds, a distance of nearly half a mile. The procession was headed by a band. Many of the pupils were in costumes and others did funny stunts. Most of the schools had banners with the names of their school on it. On the way to the grounds the different schools gave their yells. As soon as the picnic grounds were reached the sports began. They lasted all afternoon. There were many different races and other sports. Besides receiving prizes the winners of each race were awarded a certain number of points. The one who obtained the greatest number of points was given a special prize. In the evening after supper a short program was given by the pupils of the different schools. Although short it was very good. There was a large crowds. As my letter is pretty long I will now close hoping that the Pathfinders enjoyed their holidays.

                                          Russell Robinson

Clair, Sask.
Free Press Prairie Farmer
August 25, 1920

To Study Engineering

Dear Maple Leaves:

I am attending Mt. Allison Academy, and am to matriculate this year. I will then enter university and am going to study for the engineering course.

I belong to Harbour Grace, Newfoundland, and have been here at school for two years. There are four Newfoundlanders here at the academy this year and quite a number at the University Ladies' College.

We are starting to practice football now and expect to put up a fine team this year.

I would like to correspond with some girls about my own age, 16 years old. I must close now, we have to go to bed at ten here.

Mt. A. Boy

David Duff
Mt. Allison Academy
Sackville, N.B.
Family Herald and Weekly Star
October 24, 1917

A Race with an Ox

Dear Pathfinders:

This is my third letter to the club. Before we had horses we used oxen, so when I was about 12 years old I used to walk to school in the winter time. But one day I thought I'd try and go to school with an ox, so I make an old kind of stoneboat out of poplar trees, and I set an old wooden box on it and the next day I was ready for school. Well, you know, that ox could run as well as any old horse, so the next day when I got to school everybody laughed at me till one smart boy asked me if I'd take a race with him going back home, so I said yes, for I did not care if I lost or won. Well, at 4 o'clock after school, I got ready and I was gone about a half mile away before that boy was ready to start back home again; so as I was walking slowly along the road he came trotting behind me, and he shouted in a loud voice, "Get off the road," thinking I'd let him pass, so I looked around and as he was near me I shouted to him in return: "Beside the road there is a ditch and if you want to win the race you'd better jump in it." So thinking he could pass ahead of me he turned his 20-year old horse on the side of the road, but when I saw that I gave my ox a slash of the whip and away he went like a wheelless car. And the best thing that boy had to do was to get behind on the road and follow me, because his old horse was too young to win a race with a runaway ox. This is to show that an ox is sometimes better than an old horse.

Ernest Pierre (16)

Free Press Prairie Farmer
November 20, 1920

A Wheat Raiser

Dear Pathfinders:

I have been reading your letters ever since we took the paper. And I want to become a member, too. I will be 12 years old on the 7th of March. I have 3 1/2 miles to go to school. The name of my school is the Clifford school. Our school was closed in October on account of the flu. I am in the fifth grade. My teacher drove her car and I rode with her. I cranked it for her. Sometimes when it was cold we boys had to push it down the hill to get it started. We have a car. It is a Ford. I like to run a car. I have shot 12 jack rabbits and an owl this winter with a shotgun. We live nine miles from town. My papa let me have a piece of ground this year and I got 12 bushels of wheat from it. I was in the Boys' and Girls' Pig contest this summer and I got 7th prize. The prize was $4. I brought a $50 Victory Bond with my money. I have a brother that enlisted in 1916. He was killed in action on Oct. 30. He was 25 years old.

Kenneth Lyon (11)

Box 146, Admiral, Sask.
Free Press Prairie Farmer
February 12, 1919

Plate 11. Girl on pony, undated (Saskatchewan Archives Board [R-A11462]).

Plate 12. Boy with Newfoundland dog and cart, undated (Provincial Archives of Newfoundland and Labrador [A32-58]).

"I Have a Pony"
Children and Their Pets

Pets were important companions to lonely rural children. They played with them, romped with them, talked to them, and showered affection upon them. As with family members, pets were expected to contribute to family life and family income. Dogs helped handle cattle, cats caught mice, ponies and horses provided transportation and pulled farm machinery. Others animals and fowl provided breeding stock for the farm herd or poultry flock or were served up as part of the family diet. Children often attempted to tame wild birds and animals they found in surrounding woods and fields, but their captives struggled to be free and usually escaped or died in the attempt.

Pony Cut Foot

Dear Editor:

This is the first letter to the Legion of the West. I have been reading the letters in the Free Press. We have taken the Free Press seven years. I like to read Buster Brown. I have a pony. His name is Bay Niche. He is 9 years old. I go after the cattle with him every night. Once our cattle were in our neighbor's field, and I had to go and drive them out. I had to go over the barbed wire fence to get into the field. My pony caught his foot in wire and pulled back and cut his foot very bad, but we are putting medicine on it and it is getting better now. My sister received a button and I thought it was very nice, so I am going to write, hoping to get a button, too, and wishing the club success.

Cecil Olson

Starbuck, Man.
Free Press Prairie Farmer
July 8, 1908

A Funny Cat

Dear Maple Leaves:

I have a funny cat. She will eat cabbage and porridge, candy, citron, rhubarb and the cores of apples. One time I gave her some gum and she swallowed it.

I was feeding the hen and her chickens one day when the cat came along and smelt at one of the chickens. The hen flew at the cat, and the cat bit the hen on the side of the head and knocked her over. I called her the tiger cat.

She will get a stone in her front paws and lie on her back and play ball. But one time when she was doing that the hen with her chickens came along. The hen thought the cat had one of her chickens and she pecked the cat. Then the cat chased the hen into the bushes.

One evening when my sister was sent upstairs the cat hid behind the door, and when I came down she jumped at me and ripped a big hole in my dress. She plays hide-and-go-seek with me. She catches a gopher almost every day.

Anne Belle Banscmer

Lundbrech, Dutch Coulee, B.C.
Family Herald and Weekly Star
July 29, 1914

The Cat and the Baby Rabbit

My uncle had a cat which had five kittens. As he had more cats than he needed, he took them from her and drowned them, which made the poor cat feel very badly indeed.

One day not long after that, when my uncle was out in the field he found a young rabbit, and brought it home with him. The cat took possession of it and licked it with her tongue, and nursed it as if it were her own kitten.

But the cat had a habit of sleeping with my uncle and it took the rabbit upstairs to bed. Some way it got under the covers and was smothered, and that was the end of the rabbit.

Nellie Riddell (8)

Oakner, Man.
Grain Growers' Guide
February 3, 1915

Sport

I have a dog, his name is Sport. One Saturday night, about two years ago, as he was going to the barn after dark, a horse kicked him and broke his front leg. Papa was going to kill him, but we felt so bad that he would not. Mamma tied it up and kept him in the house for a month. He is very good at bringing the cows. He pulls me on the sleigh in winter.

Hazel Baily (12)

Bengough, Sask.,
Grain Growers' Guide
April 17, 1915

My Horse

I have an old horse. His name is Chub. He is twenty years old. I can do anything with him. My sister and I drive him to school sometimes. When it is real cold in the winter we cannot hold him. When I am riding him after the cows, he will bite them if they don't go as fast as he wants to go. If any of them turn out of the road he will go after them without me turning them. He will not hurt colts. My sister rides him in the winter and pulls me on a sleigh.

Robert Baily (10)

Bengough, Sask.,
Grain Growers' Guide
April 17, 1915

A Fox Farm

Dear Dixie Patton:—

My father has a fox farm and last summer we had a silver fox. One day papa went out and she had some little puppies. No one could go near her for a while. Then one day papa went down and she was carrying one of the puppies in her mouth hunting for a place to bury it, so papa got the gun and shot a rabbit for her and she forgot about her puppy. Papa found a little black fox with its head in the wire. Now we have Fluffy, the mother, and two of the young ones, the black and the cross silver also. This is a true story.

Mary A. Force (10)

Portage la Prairie,
Grain Growers' Guide
June 23, 1915

The Rabbit's Nest

One day as I was coming home with the cows I heard something making a noise as I was coming up the lane. I thought I would see what it was so I climbed thru the fence and I saw an old rabbit over by the bush so I nearly knew what it was. I saw three little rabbits so I called mother to come and see what was here. When she came we picked them up, but we put them back again. As we were going away the mother came to them and fed them. One day as father was breaking we saw a little rabbit. It nearly got under the horses' feet, so we stopped and it got out of the way.

Edna Hicks (8)

Red Deer, Alta.
Grain Growers' Guide
February 2, 1916

Rooster Named Kaiser Bill

Dear Maple Leaves:

This is my first letter to your club. We get the Family Herald every week and have taken it for more than five years. I find it the best and most interesting paper we get, and especially I like reading your letters.

I live on a farm. I have six brothers and three sisters; I am the second boy in my family; I have one brother two years older than I am, and my sister is two years younger so I have to do a lot of housework. I can do anything in a house except sew. I am fifteen years old. We live nine miles from the nearest town which is St John's.

I have several pets,—a cat, a duck, a hen, a rooster and a colt. The cat's name is Puss; the hen is Blacky; the duck is Quackie; the colt is Maude, and the rooster's name is Kaiser Bill! I name him that because he is cranky and tries to peck me when he gets a chance.

I am very fond of flowers and have over fifty different kinds. I would like to correspond with Leaves, my own age, who like flowers, poultry, and Nature. I will answer all letters or cards.

Rosebud

Bertie Stephenson
St. Luc, St. John's Co., Que.
Family Herald and Weekly Star
January 5, 1916

A Thirsty Colt

One day papa and mamma and brother and I were going to an auction sale, but I did not go the whole way. I stopped at a neighbor's home three miles from our home.

At the sale papa bought a pony whose name was Ruby.

Coming home we lost our way, but we wandered around until we found the right trail again and arrived home safely.

But one of the colts was not home. Papa went to a slough west of our house. We had a well dug in the centre of it. Sure enough there was Prince with one of his legs in the well. We went home and got some chains and hitched to him and his mother, Fannie, hauled him out. He is now a fine horse, he weighs 1800 pounds.

Della McLaren (11)

Hillsdeb, Sask.
Grain Growers' Guide
February 2, 1916

The Flying Squirrels

One day my brothers and I were out getting wood. When my brother went to cut down a hollow tree four or five flying squirrels came out and ran up the tree. First one of them darted down towards the ground then sailed up again to another tree. Then the rest went, but sailed to different trees.

We thought we would like to have a couple of them to keep, so my brother ran up to a neighbor who lived near by and got a little pail with a lid on. We punched holes in the lid so they could get air. After chasing them from one tree to another one crawled under some bark and we caught it and put it in the pail then we went after another.

We got the next one with less difficulty for when it sailed for another tree it didn't make it and I caught it just as it started to run up the tree. After we had got the two we went on getting our wood in more of a hurry for we wanted to get home to show what we had got to our parents.

When we got home we set to work at once to make them a cage. The cage was made of tin about two feet long and a foot and a half wide with a screen front. There was a little box in the corner of the cage for their nest. We put lots of feathers in so they could have a good nest. For about a week they seemed bashful and afraid, but after that at night they would go through all kinds of exercises.

After they got to doing tricks we gave them a swing and many other different things. It was amusing to watch them they were so limber and quick. We had them for over a year till one of them died, then we turned the other one loose.

S. Leslie McGinitie (14)

Tofield, Alta.
Grain Growers' Guide
January 19, 1916

Dog That Carries Messages

Dear Maple Leaves:

I am a new Leaf, and English boy, aged fifteen. I have been in Canada three and a half years. I have read your letters for nearly a year and thought I would write too. If this war isn't over by the time I am old enough I shall enlist. I will go if they will take me.

I have a cat that is eighteen years old, and a hound aged twelve,—his name is Roy. Roy will take a message from the house to anywhere on the farm if you write it on a piece of paper, and put it in his mouth. When he sees two pigs or chickens fighting he runs up to them and scares them, but will not bite them. If some one at the house gives him a orange he will take it to his master. Once he was standing at the stable door when a mare came out and kicked him on the head, and made a dent in it. When we go shooting ducks or prairie chickens Roy stops and watches us shoot, and then gets after the birds; he will go into the swamp after a duck and try to bring it out.

Last spring, in a heavy thunderstorm, one of our horses and a six month's old colt were struck by lightning and killed. I would like correspondents about my own age.

Young Farmer

Richard Bishop,
Hillside Farm, Gleichen, Alta.
Family Herald and Weekly Star
March 22, 1916

Diamond

My brother has a little white pony called "Tiny," and one morning when I woke up she had a little white-faced colt with four white legs. I thought for a long time what to call him, when one day my grandmother told me to call him "Diamond," because he had a four-cornered white spot on his right side. That was in the spring. Now, his color has changed from a kind of brown to black, but the white legs and white face have remained. In the summer I was going over to town on the pony and I wanted to leave the colt at home. So I shut him in the yard and shut the barbed wire gate. I started off, when suddenly I heard a crash and I looked behind and saw him break a big poplar post down and the gate. He cut himself on the leg, but my mother put some peroxide on it. My mother thought I had better take him along with me. So I went to town and came back and turned the pony on the prairie. After a while the cut got better.

Dugald McDougall (12)

Penhold, Alta.
Grain Growers' Guide
February 23, 1916

Owl Stole a Pigeon

Dear Maple Leaves:

This is my second letter to the club. Early one morning I was going to feed our horse and on my way to the hay shed I saw a young owl sitting on the top of the hayfork. I tried to chase him, but there was no chance of doing so and about ten minutes later he seized one of my pigeons and flew away with it, and at dinner time he returned to try to get another.

David Cartwright

Merritt, B.C.
Family Herald and Weekly Star
March 22, 1916

Found a Young Seagull

Dear Maple Leaves:

Here comes a Leaf trying to look green, although it is time to fall off.

We have started school again. I certainly enjoyed my holidays, but what I enjoyed most was a trip to a little island called Mittlenatch where we kept sheep. We have to go five miles in a motor boat. There are seagulls out there, I found a young one. I gave it to a friend, but it ran away.

Coming home we saw some black fish; they have two holes in the head to let the water out which they breath (sic) in. Some ships go around and catch them for oil.

Mawitch Chaser

Nicol Manson,
Manson's Landing
Cortez Island, B.C.
Family Herald and Weekly Star
October 26, 1916

Pigeon Pie

Dear Maple Leaves:

We live on a farm eight miles from town and three miles from school. Next fall we are going to drive two young mules to school. I often get on one of them and go for a ride. My mule's name is Jake. I am going to train him for a saddle mule. He is a good old pet. He follows you wherever you go, and when he sees you coming he brays to you.

Last summer I had forty-two pigeons, but now I only have four, as we have been having pigeon pie now and then.

I would like to correspond with any girl or boy my own age (14).

                        Sweet Fourteen

Mabel L. Burnham
Reklaw, Sask.
Family Herald and Weekly Star
March 13, 1918

Trained Crow

Dear Pathfinder-in-Chief:

I am a regular book worm. I always read the Pathfinder's letters and the stories.

My father and two brothers came here from the States seven years ago and took land. It was mostly all wooded here at that time, but the fires have burned a lot of trees. There are a great many lakes and hills around here, and last winter I caught 63 muskrats and 10 weasels.

I have a very unusual pet that is called Blackie. It is a crow that I caught when I was young and tamed it. This is the second tame crow I have had. They are very easy to tame and can laugh and imitate a chicken or a turkey to perfection.

I will be glad to hear from other Pathfinders who care to write and will answer all letters.

Arthur Press

Farmingdale, Sask.
Free Press Prairie Farmer
April 17, 1918

Plate 13. Playing house, undated (Prince Edward Island Public Archives and Records Office [3885/15]).

Plate 14. Boys Brigade Camp, 1910 (E. Brown Collection, Provincial Archives of Alberta [B. 9431]).

Plate 15. Swimming from the Old Hillsborough Bridge, 1912 (Prince Edward Island Public Archives and Records Office [2767/21]).

Plate 16. Playing school, early 1900s (Prince Albert Historical Board).

"I Want to Tell You of the Fun We Had Today"
Games, Hobbies, Clubs, and Community Events

Rural children worked hard, but they also played hard. With a minimum of materials and considerable enthusiasm and ingenuity, children created an array of toys, games, and activities. A growing number of children's groups and clubs not only taught members a code of behaviour, but also stimulated physical, intellectual, mental, and spiritual growth. Social activities and the celebration of special events and holidays often involved the entire community, and youngsters were often active participants in those gatherings.

From H.M.C.S. Niobe

Dear Maple Leaves:

Being an old member of the Club I thought I would write a few lines as I have never seen any letters from this ship.

The Niobe is the flagship of the Canadian Navy. There are about 120 boys on her, all of them in training. I will tell you how our routine runs.

At six o'clock we turn out, lash up and stow hammocks. Then we scrub decks, and at half-past seven we clean guns. At eight o'clock we have breakfast and clean into the rig of the day. Then at nine o'clock all hands fall in for inspection. After inspection all boys go to training classes; then we have dinner at twelve. At ten minutes past one, the training classes commence again. At four o'clock we have tea and our day's work is practically finished. We have supper at half-past six, and at seven o'clock we get our hammocks. All boys have to be turned in by nine, when one of the officers inspects the ship and sees that everything is all right for the night.

We were having a fine time cruising around, but out ship struck the south-west ledges of Cape Sable on July 30th and will not be able to leave Halifax until she is repaired.

Well, I will write again some time. Would like to hear from ex-members of my own age (17).

                                        Canadian Tar

Harry Franklin
H.M.C.S. Niobe
Halifax, N.S.
Family Herald and Weekly Star
January 17, 1911

Camping Episode

Dear Maple Leaves:

I want to tell you of a trip two boys from Pictou and I had last summer. We left Pictou in a row boat for Brown's Point about five o'clock, and reached there at half-past six o'clock. It was a nice bright day, so we pitched out camp near a high bank and pulled the boat up on the shore.

We got things fixed up about nine o'clock. We had a swim and got dressed. At 10 o'clock we took off our boots and coats, rolled ourselves up in a blanket and went to sleep. A little later it began to rain. It grew into a fierce gale, and as there were no woods nearby to protect us from the wind, it blew the tent over the bank into the water. We were then exposed to the rain and it was very wet. We slept under the boat till morning and rowed to Pictou, where we landed and got dry clothes.

I would like to correspond with any other Leaves my own age, age 13, also with Uncle Josh and Norman Wallace.

Tender Lou

Ivan Underwood
New Glasgow, N.S.
Family Herald and Weekly Star
June 28, 1911

The Great Debate

Dear Maple Leaf:

I am interested in the reciprocity debate, which has been taking place at the Canadian House of Commons at Ottawa, during the past session. I enjoy attending the political meetings where the question is discussed on the public platform. I would like to hear the opinion of some of the other Leaves on this important question.

I am very patriotic and my motto is "Canada for Canadians." Here are some beautiful lines which should be often repeated when the future welfare of our country is left to public opinion.

"Strong are we? Make us stronger yet;

Great? Make us greater far; Our feet Antarctic oceans fret;

Our crown the polar star; Round earth's coasts our batteries speak

Our highway is the main, We stand as guardian of the weak,

We burst the oppressor's chain."

I would like to correspond with any of the Leaves who would write first. I would also like to have a post-card shower.

Tory

W.T. Galbraith
Bluevale, Ont.
Family Herald and Weekly Star
June 28, 1911

(You have the true Canadian spirit, Tory. The Leaves should take a interest in all the concerns of Canada's life, and are very welcome to discuss such matters for the benefit of the Club, when their letters are like yours, without expression of bitterness directed against political persons. There are such expressions in some letters that have come in, and that spoils the letters. Ed.)

A Word to the Leaves

Dear Maple Leaves:

I come this time to talk on a subject that concerns most of the little Leaves of all ages and I know I can take a good share of my advice to myself, if I give any, and I intend to give a little.

It is on the subject of misbehaviour in Sunday Schools and Church services. In city—and country alike—this spirit of irreverence prevails more or less throughout our entire Dominion, and S. S. teachers amongst all classes of children agree that one of the biggest difficulties they have to contend with is this tendency to "cut up' during religious services. I am sure that if boys and girls could realize the annoyance it causes others, to say nothing of the slur it throws on themselves as well as their parents or guardians, they would not do it.

In some the fault may be lack of politeness and home training, but I think in the majority of cases it is thoughtlessness. Many of us who can be very polite and considerate when personally addressed, behave very badly in church. We, as children, young men and women, must not expect that all our battles with temptation are to be fought by our ministers and Sunday school teachers, parents and guardians. Each one of us has a responsibility that cannot be shouldered by any one else.

The glorious Christmas season is here and let us all be cheerful, and when we are making our New Year resolutions may we resolve that, although the word "selfishness" will remain in our dictionary for all time, we can do a great deal toward blotting it out of our lives through our own individual selves.

Every Inch a Boy

Man.
Family Herald and Weekly Star
January 7, 1914

What Boy Leaves Are Doing

Dear Maple Leaves:

I am going to tell you about our Boys' Club. We hold it in the United Baptist church every Monday evening. It is a part of the Boy Scout organization, and our pastor, Mr. Burnett is our master. Our motto is "Push."

We have enrolled, in all, sixteen members. The officers are president, vice-president, secretary, treasurer, chaplain, guard, and reporter. Our master gives us lessons on First Aid. We hold debates and give recitations. We go on hikes and expect to go for a sleigh-ride soon. I would like to correspond with boys or girls about thirteen years of age.

Twenty-two

Authurette, N.B.
Family Herald and Weekly Star
February 14, 1914

A Fine Coasting Tray

Dear Maple Leaves:

My sister and I have a nice coasting path, and we have fun on it in the afternoons after our lessons are done. Our mother gives us lessons every day. We have one ordinary coasting sled, two home-made barrel stave sleds, and best of all, an old iron tea tray. And oh, Leaves, it is such fun going down on the tray. You can make it spin round and round if you like, but it will go straight, too. It seems to go faster if you go down backwards; it's because you can't see in front, I expect.

We also have two pairs of skis. They go better near Spring when there is a crust on the snow.

Mariposa Lilly

Rock Creek, B.C.
Family Herald and Weekly Star
March 18, 1914

A Snow Snake

Dear Maple Leaves:

We have very cold weather here now, and lots of good ice for skating, sleighing and throwing the snow snake. Perhaps most of the Leaves have never seen a snow-snake. It is a piece of maple, eight or ten feet long, and 3/4 of an inch in circumference. It is polished very smooth and always kept polished on the bottom with tallow, and an Indian who is an expert at the game can throw it about three-eights of a mile; but we white boys are not as expert at the game as the Indians are.

We have great fun sleigh riding down hills; sometimes we hook six sleds together and with a boy on each sled away we go sailing down the hill. I am in the senior third class in school.

Farmer Boy

Middleport, Ont.
Family Herald and Weekly Star
March 18, 1914

Hallowe'en

I will tell you of the pleasant surprise that the young folk had at our house on Hallowe'en. There was a large crowd, and they gathered at the schoolhouse and all put on masks and old fashioned clothing. Some of the men dressed like women, and one girl had on bib overalls, sweater, boy's cap and mask with whiskers on, but as soon as she spoke we knew who she was.

When they first came they walked right in and didn't knock. It was about half-past eight. Papa and mamma were sitting reading, baby was playing near the door and saw them first and began to scream. It frightened her. After they were here a while papa pulled their masks off. They would run around the room trying to keep their masks from getting pulled off. After a while they took their masks off, and then we started playing games and danced a little.

They stayed until two o'clock in the morning. Two of them shook hands with me. It frightened me a little because I had never seen a mask before.

Clara Alberts

Marengo, Sask.
Grain Growers' Guide
June 10, 1914

Belongs to Girl Guides

Dear Maple Leaves:

I writing again to tell you all about the Girl Guides, whom I have joined in Grand Falls. We meet every Monday night at 7:30, in a room we have of our own. We have games of all sorts and our Captain takes us out every Saturday afternoon. In the winter she used to make signs in the snow and we had to follow them. She would also hide things in the snow for us to find. We have to salute her in the morning when we first see her.

We have been learning to cook lately. Isn't that fine? There are in all five patrols, with 13 or 16 girls in a Patrol.

                                        Mignonette

Grand Falls, Nfld.
Family Herald and Weekly Star
July 22, 1914

Lives in Evangeline's Land

Dear Maple Leaves;

I have been a silent member of this Club for three years, so I thought I would find out if there was room for me on the old tree. I live in the country which was immortalized in Longfellow's "Evangeline" and am able to see Blomidin and Grand Pre from my home.

The other day I found a belt buckle ten feet underground bearing the letters R.A.D., supposed to stand for Royal American Dragoons, a regiment which was stationed here long ago.

I suppose many of the Leaves are conversant with wireless telegraphy. A friend of mine has a set with the aerial wires 75 feet from the ground. He gets the correct time from Washington, and he got the press dispatches about the sealers who were frozen on the ice last winter. There are three sets in town, one owned by my friend and two by the Boy Scouts.

I do not agree with Clover in regard to her statement that the Nova Scotia school system is the best in the world. To teach here it is necessary to be a normal graduate or to teach only on a D certificate. You can teach only one year unless you go to Normal, so that anyone who scrapes through Normal can teach where a college president would not be allowed to.

I do not agree with Clover in regard to her statements concerning the Conservatives. Look at Sir John MacDonald and Sir Charles Tupper. And I think Sir Robert Borden did as much for Canada in refusing Reciprocity as did either Sir Wilfred Laurier or Hon. Sidney Fisher, although they have done good work.

I would like to correspond with three Leaves about my own age (16).

Basil

Family Herald and Weekly Star
August 12, 1914

A Suffragist Leaf

Dear Editor and Leaves:—

Having for a long time read your letters in silence, I also would like to join your ranks and become a Maple Leaf.

Now another Suffragette Leaf hangs from the Tree. One plea against the franchise for women is that a woman's place is in her home. I don't think her place would be very badly neglected if once in four years she left it for five minutes to cast her vote that she might help in the uplifting of humanity. No bright or intelligent women cares to be classed with idiots, lunatics and children.

May we speedily get the vote which should have been ours equally with men when the law was made.

I have studied the history of this fair Dominion of ours and I don't agree with Stick-in-the-Mud's statement that Sir John A. MacDonald was the father of Confederation. I need not say that Durham and Sewell first suggested the scheme and that afterwards in 1864 a Coalition Ministry was formed to carry Confederation. Sir J.A. MacDonald was one of the founders of the Dominion, but there were six altogether.

Just one word more. I think like everyone else that this war is a dreadful thing. Why could it not have been settled by arbitration? Think of first, the innocent lives it is taking, then the money, expense and trouble it is causing, and last of all how heathenish it is to fight.

Every success to the Club.

A Would Be Voter

Family Herald and Weekly Star
September 9, 1914

Boy Scouts' Camp Life

Dear Maple Leaves:

I saw that the editor was asking us to write and tell about our experiences while camping. I had such a good time, but did not think of keeping a logbook.

We scouts all went to the concentration camp at Penticton, B.C. There were altogether over a hundred Boy Scouts there. The first morning we got up and had breakfast before the bugler blew "cookhouse." The meals were of various kinds depending on the cook. One boy from every patrol was chosen each day.

After breakfast the bedding was aired and the camp cleaned up. This was made short work of for such a large number of boys.

The best and most useful thing was physical drill, one hour each morning.

After dinner a compulsory rest was forced and many found it hard to keep silent when not engaged in letter writing or quiet games. The thing the boys most enjoyed was leave, when everyone rushed in to town to get an ice cream or cool drinks.

The last item of the day was the camp-fire "sing-song," after which the camp was quiet and darkness.

Broncho Bill

William McGibbon
East Kelowna, B.C.
Family Herald and Weekly Star
October 6, 1915

Made Friends of the Clouds

Dear Maple Leaves:

It is nine years since I came to live on the prairie. We are twenty miles from our nearest town, and it takes us three hours to get there. When we came here first there was no trail, so we had to make one. One mark we had as a guide was a pile of stone on a hill; after that we had a gap in the hills; which helped us to keep in the right direction. Now, however, we have graded roads almost everywhere. At first we did not go to town often, but when we did we enjoyed the drive and did not think much of it. Now we think it awful to sit for three and a half hours while horses take us, so we stay at home, until it is convenient for us to go in the automobile.

Our nearest woman neighbor used to live four miles away. For days and weeks my mother, my brothers and myself were the only ones for miles around. We learned to make friends of the clouds, the birds, the flowers, the gophers, and the coyotes.

Now we go to town sometimes for a day or two. I like the music by the churches and enjoy the picture shows, but I am happiest on the prairie. Twice we have seen and helped in dreadful prairie fires. Once we had a tornado, and once a shock of earthquake. Another time I may write about these things, but I must close for now; thanking the Editor for the pretty badge which I received.

Minnehaha

Sylvia Mitchell
Neldpath, Sask.
Family Herald and Weekly Star
January 5, 1916

A Charming Play-House

Dear Maple Leaves:

I am going to tell you about our play-house at school.

One day a lot of the little girls and I went down to the remains of an old brush play-house; we thought it would be a good plan to build it up, so away we started. There were six of us to do the work.

Genia got a knife and I cut down branches while the others carried them down to the play-house. When we had enough branches we began building. We made three rooms by placing a board against a tree that formed the centre of the room. The trees growing were so arranged that they almost made a circle, and where there were no trees we cut down some and tied the branches to the trees that were growing there. When it was all finished we put in some old broken desks for chairs and tables. Then we named the rooms. One was a hall,—it had a bench, one was a parlor, and had a fireplace, a bench and a desk in it; the tiniest room was a pantry,—it had a desk to take the place of a cupboard and a table. The little girls wanted me to be mother, so I chose Fanny for the oldest, Genia for the next, Lempi came next,—then Lilly and Elsie who is only five, was the baby. We used flat stones for dishes and pretty sparkling ones for ornaments. Our broom and duster was made of branches. Everyday we clean our house and yard.

I would like to have some correspondents.

Grace Saintabin (14)

Carlin, B.C.
Family Herald and Weekly Star
January 19, 1916

Many Members at Oak Lake

(Second Prize Letter)

Our club is a branch of the Farm Boys' and Girls' club of Manitoba, organized under the direction of the Extension Department of the Manitoba Agricultural College. Our motto is, "I will never give up until I succeed." Our membership consists of about one-hundred fifty. We received one dozen eggs to set, seed potatoes and corn to plant. We also received books of instruction on tending to these things, and a note book in which we were to record our experience in the handling of them. The object of our club was to introduce pure-bred fowl and a higher grade of potatoes and corn. More important than this was the object to stimulate among the boys and girls of Manitoba an interest in the growing and tending of all three.

The first year our membership badge was a round, red button, about the size of a twenty-five cent piece, with a number in the centre to distinguish one contestant's badge from another. The second year it was about the size of a dime and was blue with a red centre. On it in little gold letters was embossed the name of the club. When the eggs were being distributed, we were given our choices of several kinds of eggs among which White Wyandottes and Rhode Island Reds received the preference. Those whose turn came last were disappointed because they had to take Buff Orpingtons. We were given seeds of all three varieties of corn, namely, Longfellow, Northwestern Dent and Gehu.

I was very unfortunate with my setting of eggs, and out of one dozen eggs which were supposed to be Buff Orpingtons, three of these were hatched and two were Black Orpingtons, if there are any.

Our club fair was held about September. Each contestant was required to show one bushel of potatoes, and a sheaf of each of the three varieties of corn, and all the poultry we had been successful enough to rear. A few days before the fair we were asked to write an account of our experiences in handling our fowl and plants, referring to our note books for facts. This we were to send to the Department at Winnipeg. At the fair points were given for it in the placing of the awards. Eventually, no matter how good the exhibits were, if the composition was poor, or one had neglected to write it, their chance of a prize was lowered a great deal. Every member was expected to show their products at the fair. Two men came up from Winnipeg to judge the array of exhibits. One of the men, at the 1915 fair, showed us how to kill a fowl and pluck it while it was warm. He did this in a very few minutes, but he also did it in the school yard, and we were picking up feathers for days afterwards. There is a rumor that the club will not be continued, but even if that is so, in a sense it will never be discontinued, because we have a start on purebred fowl and seed potatoes and corn and our motto is "I will never give up until I succeed."

Annie Taylor (13)

Oak Lake, Man.
Grain Growers' Guide
March 29, 1916

Sunshine Workers

Dear Maple Leaves:

I belong to St Albans Church. Our Sunday School class is called "Sunshine Workers." We try to be little sunbeams by helping the poor and those in trouble, and being very pleasant at home, school and everywhere.

One day my grandma had a little Guild for the Sunday School Class to learn to sew. But we can all sew better now because it was quite a while ago.

I hope some of the Leaves my own age will write to me.

                          Sunshine

Miss Bernice Delong
Carrying Place, Ont.
Family Herald and Weekly Star
March 20, 1918

Edmonton Fair

Dear Pathfinders:

Daddy and I went up to the Edmonton show two weeks ago. I took a calf up, but I didn't get a prize. There were 10 prizes offered and I came sixteenth.

We were taken to Swift's packing plant to learn about cattle. We saw some beef that had come from Sedgewick demonstration farm. I have been there, as we live 14 miles from Sedgewick. We were told that it was only pigs that we shipped overseas that were singed. We saw them singe some. They are singed to get the skin tender. They test eggs for setting and shipping the same way as we test ones at home. They have a wooden box with a hole the shape of an egg on one side. They put a lamp underneath the box. The egg to be tested is then put before the hole. If the egg is clear it is quite good.

Every night the Mounted Policemen performed at the show grounds. A peg would be driven into the ground, one at each side of the arena. Then a Mounty on horseback took a lance and picked up the peg. Next he took a lance in one hand and a sword in the other. He picked both the pegs up and waived (sic) them.

The funniest thing in the whole show was the general purpose class. There was a big Clyde mare, a black ox that was 6 ft. high if it was an inch, a Shetland pony, a car filled with hay, a man with a goat in one hand and a cream can in the other, and a mule. I don't know which won the prize.

There was also a football about 6 ft. in diameter. This was played by men who certainly were not athletes, but stout storekeepers and such like. One man got knocked down. Two other men rushed up with a bed. They picked the fallen hero up and poured red paint all over him.

I would like Hazel Withrow and Louise Carpenter to write to me.

                              Fanny E. Mundy (12)

Lougheed, Alta.
Free Press Prairie Farmer
May 1, 1918

Making a Rink

Dear Pathfinders:

    This is my third letter to your club. I have been reading them for a long time. I found them very interesting. I am going to tell about our neighbour's curling rink. The boys chose a good spot for it. There were three ponies working. All the rest had sleighs with boxes on them, and were hauling snow for the sides and ends. We flooded it about four times a day for about a week. Then we got two tanks of water. We have a little shanty with a stove in it, and it is lovely and warm when we have the fire going. There are benches in there. I would like to correspond with any boy my own age.

                                          Theodore Holden (9)

Boissevain, Man.
Free Press Prairie Farmer
January 1, 1919

The Boy Chemists

Dear Pathfinders:

I will not take up a lot of your time telling about myself but will tell you about one of my adventures. For Christmas I got a chemical outfit and I organized a Boy's Chemical club. The club progressed favorably for about two months, when Walter Hayne, librarian of our club, met with an accident.

One night as he was trying an experiment he boiled the liquid in the test tube longer than mentioned in the book, causing the tube to break. The liquid ran down his hand and over his face, burning them very badly. Being a Boy Scout, and knowing my first aid, I stopped the pain until we got him home. He is up and around now, but still unable to use his left hand. The club is under way again, and this time everybody is obeying the directions in the book.

I would like to correspond with some of the Pathfinders.

William Brown (13)

541-F Allowance Ave.
Medicine Hat, Alta.
Free Press Prairie Farmer
March 19, 1919

At the Circus

Dear Pathfinders:

I went to see the circus on the 24th of May. Daddy, my youngest sister and I went to it. There were two tents. Inside of the first one were the animals. I saw an elephant, a camel, a leopard, and a father and mother with three little baby lions. I saw in the other tent quite a few clowns and actors. There were ponies that did a drill, and goats that walked a ladder and a tight-wire. The elephant, that I saw in the other tent did a little drill. Then there were two monkeys; they had a tea-party, and then two of them played the piano.

We had a picnic down at the river last week. I went down in the afternoon. There were races, but I did not go in any of them. It had rained the night before so the roads were very muddy and bumpy. I hope to see my letter on the Pathfinders' page next week.

Marion Aikins (9)

Estevan, Sask.
Free Press Prairie Farmer
June 13, 1920

Junior U.F.M.

Dear Pathfinders:

I have not written to the page for a long time as I had nothing interesting to say, but now I have some news for you all.

The local of the United Farmers of Manitoba has been formed in our district and all the boys and girls in our school have formed a junior local and elected me president, and Pearl Elliot secretary. You all know her. It's great fun holding meetings like the grown-up folks and electing officers and passing motions.

We are making a rule that all members must join the Pathfinders' club and we are going to select a member every week to write to the Pathfinders and tell them what we are doing. We would like to have other members that belong to the United Farmers of Manitoba to write to us so we can read them at our meetings. If there is no local where you are, you'd better form one. Our local is called Park View Local, Junior section. This letter is getting too long, so, although I have lots more to tell you, I must cut my letter short.

Pete Whitall

Lesdale, Man.
Family Herald and Weekly Star
March 22, 1920

Plate 17. Ojibway girl cleaning fish, Missanabie, Ont., 1903 (A. A. Chesterfield Collection, Queen's University Archives, Kingston, Ontario).

Plate 18. Young boy with caribou, undated (Provincial Archives of Newfoundland and Labrador [A17-176]).

"I Have Been Trapping This Year"
Hunting, Trapping, and Fishing

What more could an adventurous rural youngster desire than a fishhook and a line, a rifle, and a few traps? Wildlife abounded in nearby streams, woods, and fields. It was there for the taking. But fishing, hunting, and trapping were more than sport. Youngsters augmented family larders with the fish they caught, the wild fowl they shot, and any larger game they were able to bring down. They augmented family income with money earned from the sale of the furs from their traplines. But hunting and trapping were not without danger, and on occasion children were injured or killed through the careless use of firearms.

Shot Many Gophers

Dear Editor.

    I received my button, and I think it is just beautiful. I thank you very much for it. My uncle Tom, and my brother Jimmie and I were out hunting gophers yesterday. We shot about 20, and snared some. We were hunting nearly all day. I like hunting; it is great sport. I will close, wishing the club every success.

George Still

Orrwold, Man.
Free Press Prairie Farmer
July 22, 1908

Going Fishing

I arose just as the sun came peeping over the eastern hills. It shone on the dew-laden cobwebs and made them sparkle and glisten, so they appeared like silver plates on the grass.

After eating my breakfast I went out to the stable to help my father do the chores which included feeding the horses, milking the cows and such like.

After they were done I came back to the house to get ready to go fishing. My mother tied me up a lunch. Then securing my fishing outfit, I started across the fields to where a friend of mine lived. We had made arrangements some time before to go fishing. I found him all ready so we started at once.

As we walked along we noticed all the different kinds of birds. They were all singing their very best as if they knew it was the Queen's Birthday. The squirrels were playing hide and seek in the woods, and now and then a sly old woodchuck would take a peep at us out of the top of a hollow stump or around a log.

At last, after a long walk, we arrived at the fishing pond. We had good success, as we caught a large number of bass and several other kinds. At noon we found that we had all the fish we could carry home.

Under the shade of a near-by maple tree we ate our lunch. We then wandered about in the adjoining woods until it was time to go home. It was not until late in the afternoon that we arrived home, tired, but in every other respect feeling none the worse for the holiday.

Frank Johnson (14)

Manchester, Ont.
Family Herald and Weekly Star
August 2, 1911

The Deer Fever

Dear Maple Leaves:

No objections to a newcomer, dear Editor, even though he isn't one of the bunch as the saying goes? I like to read the letters in the M.L.C. corner. That's the page I look for as soon as I get the paper and enjoy them very much. We live on a farm here in Northern Ontario, and like it fine, although it is now getting cold. Old Jack Frost is making his presence felt now, especially in the mornings. Just think of all the pleasures we derive from him. They are too numerous to mention.

We have great times here going out setting snares for rabbits. We go out on snowshoes, which gives us great pleasure also. My dad and I each shot a deer this season. My brother was with us, and had a nice chance to get one, too, at one time, but he took what we call deer-fever. He got excited. When he saw the deer so close he threw the gun down and made for the deer with outstretched arms. Of course you know the result; Mr. Deer was away like a shot.

I am going to college next spring. Father says he is tired of having me at home doing nothing. He's mean, don't you think so, Editor? We must obey him, though, eh? for he knows what is best for us.

I have a fine hound and a spaniel. Have great times with them. We found a bear last week, my brother and I. We were out looking at our snares, and Jack (that's my hound) smelt him, I guess. We didn't bother Mr Bruin. We kind of took cold feet and retraced our steps.

I believe I've written enough for my first time, for I know what Mr. or Miss Editor will do to such trash. If it doesn't reach that dreadful W.P.B. as most of the Leaves call it, well—I might come again with the goods. So I won't trouble you longer, dear Editor.

Buttinsky

Family Herald and Weekly Star
January 17, 1912

What I Do

Dear Maple Leaves:

I am a sportsman like some of the members; my favorite occupations are riding horseback, boating, hunting and trapping. I have a twenty-two rifle and revolver; also a breech-loading shotgun. I trap coon, weasel, muskrat and skunk, and I shoot and snare a large number of rabbits. I have read such books as "The Blazed Trail," "Strive and Succeed," "Andy Grant's Pluck" and many others. I am now reading the new serial in the Star and think it is a good one. I would like to hear from anyone of the Leaves who will find my name with the Editor.

An Outlaw

N.S.
Family Herald and Weekly Star
February 25, 1914

A Caribou Hunt

Dear Maple Leaves:

    I am going to tell you about a caribou hunt that grandfather and I had last summer. We started from home at half-past three in the morning of August 3rd; we travelled all day and we put up our camp in the evening to spend the night. Next morning we awoke early and after breakfast started to look for caribou. We went up a river and made for high ground where we could see a long way across country. At last we saw two caribou and then we made for the river again. We got near enough to one of them—a stag, and my grandfather fired and killed him. Then we skinned him and took a piece each and started for home.

    My two uncles left the next morning and brought the remainder of the meat home.

    I would like hear from my old correspondents.

                                  Young Hunter

Ernest Gosneg
Black River, Placentia Bay, Nfld.
Family Herald and Weekly Star
April 13, 1914

Large Catch

Last summer my parents, brothers, and sister and I went camping by a lake a little distance from our home, called Sandy Lake. There is a little village on the south shore. We camped about a half a mile east of it.

We did quite a lot of fishing, and one beautiful evening my two brothers, my father and I went out fishing. We had three fishing hooks, two new ones and one old one which did not catch fish. We each wanted a new one, but my father said, "Whoever will take the old one will have good luck."

I took the old one, and before we had gone a hundred yards I felt a tug on my line. I at once began pulling it in, but it pulled so hard I was letting my line go out all the time. It just about pulled me out of the boat, and then I gave the line to father, who pulled it up to the boat. We then saw it was a big fish, and he gave me the line while he rowed ashore. Some campers came running along the shore, and one man gave it one hit with a stick and it was killed. When we reached town we found it weighed sixteen pounds.

This really happened to me while on my holidays at Sandy Lake.

Mabel Peacock

Newdale, Man.
Grain Growers' Guide
April 22, 1914

Untitled

I will tell a true story. I was going through the bush along the creek when I heard a loud noise in the water and as I drew near I saw a large beaver and three smaller ones, so I sat down to see what they would do. The old beaver went up on the side of the hill and started chewing at the willow. When he got his mouth full he let it drop out. Soon he had the tree cut and the little one started eating leaves and smaller branches. Then Mr. Beaver took the largest branches and carried them down and under the water. When the tree was all gone the beavers went under the water and I saw them no more until the next day. I will soon be seventeen. My pen name is

Farmer Boy

Legion of the West
Free Press Prairie Farmer
August 12, 1914

A Horsewoman

Dear Maple Leaves:

How many Maple Leaves like trapping? Although I am a girl I can set traps just as well as my brother and can also shoot. This winter my brother is trapping and he has already caught four wild cats. He took a photo of one and I am going to send it in this letter. I was with him when he was taking the photo and the wild cat was growling and trying to get loose. It was a wonder it did not because it was only caught by two toes. He has not caught any coyotes yet because they are so hard to catch. Not very long ago a coyote set one of the traps off, ate the bait and went away.

How many of the Leaves like to ride tricky horses? I just love to, just for the fun of getting the better of them. I also love racing and have a bay mare that I race very time I get the chance. She likes to go and I have never been beaten yet. Once you have raced her she gets excited and if you do not let her run she stands on her hind legs and paws the air. She is also a pretty good trotter. She can go five miles in 26 minutes in a two-wheeled cart. Even then I did not let her go as fast as she wanted to and besides I had five gates to open on the way. She also does all kinds of tricks, such as kissing, shaking hands, putting her paw-feet up on a rock when told, and pawing the ground when you tap her on the shoulder, keeping time to whatever music you are singing.

Maggy

Another nameless, address-less letter. Write again, Maggy, and show us that you keep the rules.—Editor.

Family Herald and Weekly Star
January 27, 1915

Climbing over Icebergs

I am fourteen years of age and live in a small settlement in the northern part of Newfoundland. I think some of the Leaves would be surprised to hear that in the month of June we can go out and climb over great icebergs. I have a small gun and my friend and I often go out on the ice to look for young seals. My friend shot one the other day, it was great sport. I go to school and when I have finished school I intend to go fishing with my father. My father does quite a bit of gardening and grows a great many vegetables. In the next letter that I write I will tell you about an adventure I had last winter

I love sport and dancing.

                                                  Graball

Ambrose Thistle
Island Hr., Nfld.
Family Herald and Weekly Star
October 18, 1915

A Terrible Sight

Dear Maple Leaves:

    I am going to tell you of an experience I had with a bear. A short time ago, while I was out hunting for partridge I got a terrible fright. After shooting one partridge and giving up hope of seeing any more, I started for home. When I was near the edge of the woods where there is rocky cliff I heard some heavy beast crunching and breaking the limbs as he walked along. The bush was so thick that I could not see what it was. I bent down and then I got the greatest surprise of my life. There he was! A great big brute of a bear walking along! As I was only a few hundred feet away from home it did not take me long to get there. It was a good thing that the bear did not notice me. He was carrying something but I was so frightened that I could not tell what it was he had. Anyhow, I hope I won't get so frightened again.

    Will some of the girls, of my own age (15), write and send me the words of an old song "The Old Log Cabin Down the Lane."

The Little Hunter

John McClean
Ohio, Antigonish Co., N.S.
Family Herald and Weekly Star
January 26, 1916
You were very nearly the hunted that time, Little Hunter.—Editor.

Shooting of Sand Hill Cranes

Dear Maple Leaves:

I have been reading the letters on your page for a long time, and at last got the courage to write a letter myself. I want to be another Leaf on the tree.

I hope I shall see my letter in print as this is my first experience of writing to a paper or a club.

Quite a lot of you wrote about the wild geese and ducks going South, but none of you said anything about the Sand Hill Cranes going away. They are all gone now, but there were thousands in this neighborhood last fall, but when it began to be rather cold at nights they flew away to their winter haunts. They raise their young here in the summer time. I shot one with my 22-in. rifle; it is only a cool person with lots of patience that can shoot them, as they have such long necks, and they can see a long way off; also there is always one on the lookout all the time; sometimes you have to creep half a mile before you can get a shot at them. I have lots of practice at creeping up at them, and had to wait patiently for seven or eight hours before I could get near enough to shoot at them.

I came from Scotland three years ago last July, and am glad too, as they are having real hardships to face over there now. I would like to get correspondents as I am very lonely at times. I will answer all letters promptly, whether it be girls' or boys'. I am fourteen years of age.

           Bonnie Scotland

William Allan
Smithburg via Davidson, Sask.
Family Herald and Weekly Star
January 10, 1917

Skins Paid for Bond

Dear Pathfinders:

I would like to join your club and am sending the coupon. I am in Grade VIII. We live two and a half miles from school. Our school is closed now on account of the flu. We have traps set for coyotes and we got one this morning. Last year we sold $50 of coyote and muskrat hides, so we bought a victory bond. I am sending a drawing of "Little Red Riding Hood." I will close now hoping to see my letter in print.

Ethel Place (14)

Viking, Alta.
Free Press Prairie Farmer
January 8, 1918

The Slimy Octopus

Dear Pathfinders:

    I am going to tell you a story about an octopus Mr. Martin, a fisherman up here caught in his net today. It was quite big and it looked kind of like a jelly-fish. It seemed to be all colors; it was red, blue and gray, and it had a little bit of white in it. It had about seven long arms. Its skin hung loose and slimy around it. It had two rows of suckers underneath these fearful arms. Its mouth is underneath its head. When I saw it I thought it had been skinned. Daddy said he drove a nail into one of its arms and it just drew itself away as easy as possible and left the nail in the board. Mr. Martin tied a rope around its neck and then to a post. It pulled so hard to get away that it choked itself. I have been (reading) the Book of Knowledge and I just read in it about an octopus that had eyes a foot in diameter and had a head that would hold three hundred and fifty gallons. I would not like to be close to one that size, would you? If any of the Pathfinders have seen an octopus would they please write to me. I will answer all letters.

                                  Marjorie Hopwood (12)

Blubber Bay, B.C.
Free Press Prairie Farmer
March 19, 1919

Nearly Killed by Shot

Dear Pathfinders:

This is my first letter to your club. I read the letters every week and think they are very interesting. I was shot in the stomach and went to Holy Cross hospital in Calgary. While I was there my sister sent the paper to me.

I was in hospital for three weeks. They were very good to me, but I do not like it in the hospital. I just got home yesterday. I was shot on the 24th of July. I have to stay in bed nearly all the time, but I can walk some with some one to guide my feet. No one expected me to live, as we live twenty-two miles from the nearest doctor's place. He told us to go to Calgary.

Bruce Bell (9)

Carvath Corner, Alta.
Free Press Prairie Farmer
September 8, 1920

Plate 19. The blacksmith shop, undated (Provincial Archives of New Brunswick [(m11) 432]).

Plate 20. Lobstery cannery, Fortune, P.E.I., undated (Prince Edward Island Public Archives and Records Office [2320/22-10]).

"My Father Is Both Fisherman and Farmer"
Occupations and Vocations

Families living in rural areas were engaged in a variety of occupations, including fishing, farming, sealing, trapping, tending lighthouses, logging, and mining. Others were employed in the construction and operation of expanding rail and road systems and in the building of growing urban centres. Children were very aware of the occupations in which their parents and neighbours were engaged. When they were big enough, and where it was appropriate, they helped with the work.

Sent a Story

Dear Editor:

This is my second letter to your club. I received my button, which was very nice. I am going to send you another story about Molly. There was a picnic here June 30. I went to it and had a fine time. My father is a blacksmith, and we keep a boarding house. I am in grade four and 11 years old. We are having beautiful weather now. I can ride a bicycle. I think I will close for this time.

Harry Dearing

Moose Park, Man.
Free Press Prairie Farmer
July 22, 1908

The Coming of the Seals

Dear Leaves:

In my last letter I told you about the coming of the harp seals. They came again last spring and with them the little baby seals only a few days old. If the Leaves could only have seen them, they would have been as excited as if they were seeing Santa Claus coming through the air on his ship.

Every one who could get on the ice was there. When the ice comes to the land it rushes together in great heaps—we call them rifters—and it was very hard getting the seals over it to land. Every man had a different tale to tell of his adventures when they came home that night.

The old seals are very fierce. The seals would fight them off. My father went out on his snowshoes, for the ice was very bad. The snowshoes tripped him up and he fell on his back just as an old seal was coming for him with open jaws. He had to strike it with his gaff before he could get up.

The young seals are yellowish at first, but in a few days they bleach white as snow and are white for about twenty days. Then the white fur comes off and black hair comes out.

                                          Mary Decker

Cape Onion, Nfld.
Family Herald and Weekly Star
August 26, 1914

Seal Fisheries

Dear Maple Leaves:

I would like to say a few words about the Newfoundland Seal Fisheries. My father was captain of the steamer "Samuel Blendford,"—he shared a very good trip in which they caught a very large number of seals.

I am trying for the Primary Grade this year and I hope I shall not fail, but it is hard to tell.

I like the Boys' and Girls' page very much.

Newfoundlander Sealer

Roland Winsom
Wesleyville, Nfld.
Family Herald and Weekly Star
July 19, 1916

A Cheesemaker's Son

Dear Maple Leaves:

I have never seen any letters from a cheesemaker's son or from this part of Ontario. I live twenty miles from Ottawa and one hundred miles from Montreal. My father is a cheese-maker. I help in the factory on Monday because that is the hardest day in the week because there is Sunday's milk as well as Monday morning's.

I tried the Junior High School entrance examinations this year but do not know whether I passed or not. I can imagine the Editor smiling at this when he sees my poor writing.

I have a collection of several thousand stamps. They are from all the continents and from nearly every country.

I am learning to swim, but can only swim five or six strokes at a time.

Some time ago I asked for correspondents in Africa, Australia or New Zealand. I did not get one correspondent. I would now like to correspond with anybody in Africa, Australia, and North of Ireland and with Edward F. Cunliffe of Trinidad. Hoping to see this letter in print.

Roydan Olmstead

Bear Brook, Ont.
Family Herald and Weekly Star
August 12, 1914

Lives in a Mining Camp

Dear Maple Leaves:

I have been a reader of this interesting Club for a long time, enjoying the letters, but have never plucked up enough courage to write until now.

I live in the Rossland mining camp, where a vast crowd of men are digging up the ore from mines and getting it ready for Trail smelter. This smelter takes from the ore, gold, silver, copper, and lead and transfers it in large blocks to the refinery where it is made into gold and silver bricks. The McGill mining students come to work in the mines during their summer holiday. We have people here of every nationality. I see some of the Leaves describe themselves. I am rather tall, have red hair and freckles. The latter I am very proud of.

My hobby is stamp collecting and I should like to exchange with anyone similarly interested. I would like to correspond with four Leaves if they will please write to me first. My age is twelve.

Soldier Boy

Gilbert Steves
Rossland, B.C.
Family Herald and Weekly Star
September 23, 1914

A New Member

Dear Editor:

I do not belong to the Maple Leaf club, but I would like to as my father takes the Family Herald and Weekly Star and has been taking it for eleven years and I read all the letters.

I am a little Indian girl, aged nine years, and I also go to school. I am in the fourth reader. My father is a trapper and a hunter. He has a mink farm and if the boys and girls would like to hear about it and the little baby mink, I may tell them sometime.

The war—well, it is a sad thing! How the Germans have used the poor children of Belgium!

I won't say anymore this time but say good-bye from

Your little Indian friend,
Lucy Charles

Family Herald and Weekly Star
December 16, 1914

Fisherman and Farmer

Dear Maple Leaves:

I live in a little place in the country called Cow Bay. It is very quiet here in winter, but in the summer crowds of people come down here from the city on picnics and go bathing. I live ten miles from Halifax.

My father is both a fisherman and a farmer. We have a gas boat for fishing. I like being in the boat when it is calm. My father and oldest brother are making traps now for lobster fishing, in the spring.

I go to school and am in the seventh grade. My reading book is Evangeline, which I think is a lovely story. I like going to school very much.

Blue Eyes

Mabel Osborne
Halifax, N.S.
Family Herald and Weekly Star
March 24, 1915

Silver Scales of the Herring

Dear Maple Leaves:

I am going to tell you about where I live. I live very close to the Atlantic Ocean and can see all the big foreign steamers and vessels that go past. My father is a fisherman, he has a gasoline boat. He catches lobsters in winter and spring, and fishes cod in the summer.

Sometimes I go with him to set his herring nets. Last summer the herrings were close by the shore so I could see them when he was setting the nets. They looked so pretty with their silver scales shining in the water. I like to go with my father to set his nets very much, and also to see the pretty herrings in the water.

I got one correspondent from Newfoundland and would like to correspond with a member from England, or anyone else of my own age (13) who wishes to write.

Winter Bird

Eva Tupper
East Side, Port L'Hebert
Queen's Co., N.S.
Family Herald and Weekly Star
June 16, 1915

Mail by Dog Team

Dear Maple Leaves:

I am eleven years old and have one sister older than I am. I like school very much.

We have lots of fun here in the winter time, snowballing, skating and sliding. This place is in the north, so it is very cold in winter. We get two mails a week, which comes by dog team. It is very much warmer in summer when the ice is all thawed out and the steamer gets around. It won't be long before we shall be able to get our mail by steamer. This is a very pretty harbor, and we go boating and berry picking and enjoy ourselves very much.

I wonder how many Leaves like the country. I would rather live in a little harbor like this than in a big noisy city.

I would be pleased if one of the girl members would write to me.

           Marguerite

Gladys Tucker
Harry's Harbor, Notre Dame Bay, Nfld.
Family Herald and Weekly Star
August 18, 1915

Blueberries as Big as Beans

Dear Maple Leaves:

I saw a lot of beautiful letters in the MLC and thought I would like to correspond with all the boys and girls.

My father is a section Foreman and I have a great time. I live in the section house which we get rent free,—we don't have to pay rent on anything.

I go to school, but sometimes I have to stay home and make hay. I have lots of sports in the winter. I hunt rabbits and sleigh ride and snowshoe and play war.

In the summer we play baseball and swim, pick blueberries and a lot of other things. There is a great big blueberry patch where the berries are as big as beans.

I would like to correspond with boys and girls (aged fourteen).

Kenneth Goodfellow

T.N.O. Railway, Ramore, New Ontario
Family Herald and Weekly Star
August 30, 1916

Felling Huge Trees

Dear Maple Leaves:

I live in the famous Fraser Valley of British Columbia. Three railroads run through the valley, one of them the British Columbia Electric Railway, runs by home. The other two are the Canadian Pacific, which runs on the other side of the Fraser River, and the Canadian Northern, which run on this side of the river.

The tall fir trees out here are very numerous, and they are very big trees, some of them being seven feet thick, of course, others are smaller. When they cut one down they use spring boards which they place in a small cut in the tree about four or five feet from the ground, and two men stand on these boards, with an eight or ten foot saw, and cut the tree down.

In the fall a large number of salmon come up the Fraser river to spawn; after they have finished spawning they return, but on their way they appear to get lost and go up some of the inland streams. After a time they get some disease and die, then they get washed up on the shore.

I would like to correspond with a girl or boy my own age (12).

Allboy

Lawrence McDermid
Coglan, B.C.
Family Herald and Weekly Star
January 10, 1917

Near Logging Camp

Dear Maple Leaves:

We live on a farm on the coast of B.C. in a place called Kingcome Inlet.

We live near a big logging camp. The railway for bringing logs to the beach is nearly eight miles long.

There are two mail boats come here every week in the summer.

I can run a little gasoline boat we have, but we have a bigger one I haven't learned to run yet.

If any Leaves will write I will answer their letters.

Launch

T. Ernest Halliday
Kingcome Inlet, B.C.
Family Herald and Weekly Star
October 10, 1917

On Lake Superior

Dear Maple Leaves:

    This is a small village on Lake Superior, and our home is just a few steps from the water.

    It is very hilly here and the Canadian Pacific Railway passes through, winding in among the hills.

    We have a coal plant here, and in summer coal-boats come in with coal. It is unloaded here and then it is used along the line. Some are American boats and some Canadian.

    I would like very much if some of the Leaves would write, and I promise to answer all letters or cards.

                              Among the Hills

Dora Almos
Jack Fish, Ont.
Family Herald and Weekly Star
October 10, 1917

Untitled

Dear Ex-Leaves;

I am an English girl. I came out from England with my parents about twelve years ago, and during that time have been to several places in Ontario.

We are living on the Sheshewaning Indian Reserve on Manitoulin Island at present and find it very lonesome. Father is a school teacher and missionary here. We have twenty-five children at this school.

We have a number of cousins and friends and also an uncle in the British Army, but have adopted two soldiers in the Canadian Army.

Nin Gwanatchiw

Irene Weeks
Family Herald and Weekly Star
December 5, 1917

Watching the Boats

Dear Maple Leaves:

I live by the Fraser River. We have ten acres of land. And my dad follows fishing in the river.

I like to watch the boats fishing. It is fun to watch the boats lined up along the river on Sunday nights, waiting for the gun to go off at 6 o'clock. Then they throw out their nets, hundreds of them at once, then they fish all week until Friday night at 12 o'clock. Then the weekly close season comes until Sunday night at 6 o'clock.

I would like to correspond with any girl my own age (11).

Fishermaid

Rene Cosulick
Ladner, B.C.
Family Herald and Weekly Star
August 14, 1918

Untitled

Dear Maple Leaves:

I have two big sisters training to be nurses; one is now finishing her course at New York after being at the Riverdale Isolation Hospital, Toronto, for three years and the other has put in a year at the same hospital.

Mother set five hens and there are fifty-five chickens. I hope they will all grow big and that we will have lots of eggs after a while.

There are some woods not far from where I live and we go get nice wild flowers.

One of the teachers who used to be here is now in a machine gun crew in France, and I hope he won't get killed. I have three dolls, Grumpy, Beauty, and Gladys.

Snow Drop

Mabel Pomfrey
Nairn Centre, Ont.
Family Herald and Weekly Star
May 12, 1918

Plate 21. A prairie home, ca. 1912 (Boissevain Community Archives, Coll. 118, Provincial Archives of Manitoba [N390]).

Plate 22. Potato picking on the Brooks' farm, Gladstone, Man., 1916 (Jessop Collection, Coll.133, Provincial Archives of Manitoba [N3174]).

Plate 23. Ukrainian family harvesting, 1918 (Dr. G. E. Dragan Collection, Public Archives of Canada [PA 88504]).

Plate 24. Gathering eelgrass, undated (Public Archives of Nova Scotia [PANS N-2066]).

"I Shall Be a Farmer"
Life and Work on the Farm and Ranch

The operation of farms and ranches engaged the entire family in a daily round of chores and a cycle of seasonal work and activities. Preparation of the land, seeding, harvesting, and the care of livestock were generally the responsibility of males. Managing the house, raising poultry, tending gardens, separating milk, making butter, and storing and preserving meat, vegetables, and fruit were the domain of women. Girls not only helped their mothers, but in some circumstances, also drove teams pulling mowers, rakes, and binders. They helped with stooking and stacking grain and hay. When necessary, boys helped mothers with cooking, cleaning, and gardening. Children listed with pride the skills they had mastered and the work they did about the farm.

Untitled

Dear Editor:

I have just found the first anemone of the season, and I thought I would tell the boys and girls of the club. This is my first spring in the west, so it [was] the very first prairie anemone I ever saw, and it was so funny, for it was growing up, right out of the snow. I thought it was pretty brave to come out when the north wind was blowing, so cold that I needed my mittens, but it had a warm, comfortable little furry hood, and whenever it got cold it just drew its hood over its head and went to sleep. I am watching every day to see what flower will bloom next. I am going to keep a list of the names of flowers just as I find them.

Flower-lover

Free Press Prairie Farmer
May 15, 1907

Grows Many Flowers

Dear Editor:

    I wrote to the Legion of the West some time ago, but I did not see it in print, so I will try again. I thank the editor very much for the button which I received not long ago. I am the only one around here that has a button. I see Etta Bull says in her letter what she would like to be so I will do so too, I would like to be a teacher. I like the profession. I have flowers such as sweet peas, pansies, nasturtiums, fox glove, sweet William. How many of the members have a garden? I like to go out picking berries. Every year we go out picking strawberries, raspberries, pincherries, chokecherries, and June berries. We have a cream separator and milk eleven cows. My brother has a farm of his own on which he is living. He lives six miles south of where we live. My father put up a large frame house last summer, brick veneered. It is the finest house around this part of the country, so many people say. I live twelve miles from the city of Saskatoon. My mother has 30 little turkeys, 220 little chickens, and a few ducks. I am a post card collector and I have about 25 cards. If any of the members would like to exchange or correspond with me, I should be pleased to answer if they write first. If Mary McDougall, St Louis, Sask. sees this letter, I hope it will remind her that she owes me a letter. I do hope that this letter is not too long, also that it will escape the waste paper basket, as the other one went into it. I will close now. Wishing the club and editor continued success, I remain

                              Dorothy Snuda

Free Press Prairie Farmer
July 22, 1908

A Good Worker

Dear Maple Leaves:

This is my third letter to the Club and as yet none have been printed, but I am going to try again.

I am a girl fourteen and one half years old, and am in the ninth grade at school, but this past year I have been home learning to do general housework. Although I am a girl, I can milk, harness a horse, and rake with a horse as well as any boy. Last year I raked about one hundred tons of hay. We have thirty sheep, forty-two head of cattle and seven horses.

I would like to correspond with June and Scotch Thistle, if they would please write first. My address is with the editor.

Farmer Lass

Family Herald and Weekly Star
May 13, 1914

An Ambitious Young Farmer

When I get older I shall be a farmer and just have registered stock. I wish I was a little older so I could raise a crop of grain for the soldiers. I will farm the old way—I will plow about six inches deep. I will also have four or five workmen. I will have pigeons, ducks, pigs, horses, cows and all mixed farming.

I will go to the agricultural college first, so I won't start backwards.

I am going to make my farm beautiful with fruit trees and nice plants around our house. I will go to fairs to see how others farm.

Jesse Welte (10)

Grain Growers' Guide
April 28, 1915

The Turkeys and the Wolves

About seven or eight years ago, when we first came to this country, there were a great many wolves around here. Some mornings when my brothers went to the barn they would hide under the binder, drill, disk and other machinery. Some mornings there was one and other mornings two, but when they would take the gun out they were not there.

In front of our house there is a great big slough, about thirty feet wide and a lot longer. Around the slough there is generally quite a lot of grass, but hardly any bushes. The wolves would hide in the places where the grass was thickest.

One year my mother had about six or seven old turkey hens and about forty young ones. These turkeys would go away to the far side of the slough to hunt bugs and grasshoppers.

After living here for some time the wolves got more scarce and more frightened, so they did not come in the yard, they waited for the turkeys to come and hunt for their food. Everyday there would be a few missing, but we had so many we did not miss them so much.

But one day my mother and I were digging the potatoes and putting them in bags. When we had just nicely started at our work two of the old turkeys came with about fifteen young ones. They walked around where we were digging the potatoes and afterwards walked quite a distance from us. When we were at the end of the patch a wolf came running. He saw the turkeys and started after them. The turkeys got scared and started to fly, but before they had run away the old turkeys told the small ones to sit down in the grass and hide and that they were not to peep. This they said in their own language, which I could not understand.

Then the old turkeys swam across the slough and ran to the barn, making an awful noise.

When I saw the turkeys fly I ran and hollered at the wolf. He ran a little distance and sat down to look at me. As I was quite small I did not go very far as I was afraid of him.

After my mother and I were thru talking about it we went to hunt the little turkeys. We hunted a few minutes and found very nearly them all. When we could not find any by walking we stood very still, then one would perhaps squeak and then we would find it. Then we would call them and find a few more. When we had them all but one or two we went to the barn and took them to the old turkeys, putting them all together in a coop.

When it got near suppertime and the men came in to eat, we told them about the turkeys and the wolf, but they only laughed.

A couple of months later, when the turkeys were on the far side of the slough, the wolf took them all but one old hen and gobbler, and about eight or nine little ones. This time the young turkeys were too big to hide, so the wolf caught them.

The next year my mother did not raise so many turkeys, as she said the wolves would only get them. However, one old turkey went back of the house in the grain with her young ones and the wolf took her and all the small ones, at least we thought he did because we found one little turkey, but that was all.

This is a true story.

Grace Koechintz (13)

Antler, Sask.
Grain Growers' Guide
October 13, 1915

Bringing Home the Cows

Dear Maple Leaves:

I live on a farm near the Bay of Fundy; it is lovely here in the summer to sit on the bank and see the fishing boats coming in, and also to watch the beautiful sunsets.

I would like some of the Leaves who live on farms to write to me. Do any of you have to go and fetch the cows on summer evenings? I do and think it is grand going through the woods,—to see the rabbits running away from your path, to hear the dear birds singing and watch the squirrels jumping from branch to branch.

I would like to correspond with boys and girls my own age (16).

Brown Eyes

Helen Hussey
Marden, N.S.
Family Herald and Weekly Star
June 14, 1916

Sheep Raising

Dear Maple Leaves:

Here is another Leaf that would like to join your club.

Three years ago I had fifteen dollars saved and I bought three sheep. Now I have got fourteen.

Last year I sold my wool and got twenty-five cents a pound. This year I have become a member of the wool growers association so will get a better price for my wool this time.

I would like to correspond with any girl my own age (14).

Goodbye dear Leaves and Editor.

                              Western Sheep Girl

Mabel Birks
Westlock, Alta.
Family Herald and Weekly Star
August 29, 1917

Billy

Dear Maple Leaves:

You see it rained awfully hard this morning and we had to stop haying so the boys took advantage of the wet weather and went to town.

I wish you could see our crew. It consists of three boys, my mother, father and myself. Mother looks after the rest of us when we get hungry, and the rest of us each do something in the fields. We expect to have one hundred fifty tons of hay this year, but will all enjoy putting it up.

The boys have christened me Billy because as skirts are so awkward I wear overalls.

All the rest of you Leaves seem to be pretty busy with your gardens. I hope they turn out successfully.

Does anyone know anything of one of the Leaves, Kitchener O'Brien?

I gained a lovely lot of correspondents the last time I wrote and hope girls and boys, of my own age, will write. Also will some Maple Leaf soldier write to

                        A Cariboo Girl

Cariboo Ranch
Beaver Lake, B.C.
Family Herald and Weekly Star
October 19, 1917

A Young Rancher

Dear Pathfinders:

    I live in the country, 34 miles from our nearest town, on the banks of the Saskatchewan River. I am in the fourth grade at school, but I am not going to school at present. We were here two years ago before we had school all the time. I have a pony named Maude. We had her for many years, and by harnessing her, I have learned to be quite a cow-puncher. I also have a cow and calf, so I think I have a pretty good start for ranching. When we first came here, nine years ago, we could hear the coyotes howling all the time. Papa drove oxen and it took him a week to go to town, so mamma baked a box of pancakes, milled a pig and filled a cider keg with coffee for his lunches. I have four sisters and two brothers. One brother, two years older than I am, herded 300 head of cattle on the river banks, and it would take him till dark to round up his cattle. Will anyone interested in ranching please correspond with me? I will answer all letters.

                                        Malnord Sandvold (10)

Ardkenneth, Sask.
Free Press Prairie Farmer
January 29, 1918

A Young Farmerette

Dear Maple Leaves:

I live on the prairie, on a farm. Among the animals on the farm my favorite is the horse. I like to ride horseback.

One morning we saw the sun shining on a elevator in the town of Millicent, thirty miles away, and some clear mornings we see the smoke from trains

They are making a new railway just five miles from here. I like to see them grading. They have sixteen horses to pull the grader.

I like to help harvest the grain and put up hay, I do a lot of it when I am out of school. I especially like to buck the hay in the stack.

My brother and I bucked in five large stacks last year. I also shocked (sic) twenty acres of grain last year myself and will have more to do this year. I, like the rest of the Leaves, have cousins in the war, but none of my brothers are old enough to go. I am trying do my share on the farm.

                          Dode

Dorothy C. Dawson
Winnington, Alta.
Family Herald and Weekly Star
October 14, 1918

A Description of the West

Dear Maple Leaves:

I would like to become a Leaf if you have no objections. Everett, my brother, and my sister Vera, are both Leaves, so I do not like to be left out in the cold. Everett has received so many beautiful cards and letters from the Leaves, that I would like to exchange cards too. I am twelve years old.

One of the Eastern Leaves wondered why Western Leaves did not describe the West, so I will try to give a slight description of our country. This is not what you call a level prairie, as it is inclined to be a little rolling. We have different methods of farming here. A few use oxen, others horses, and quite a number gasoline engines, while we must not forget the steam outfits. Naturally the oxen are a little bit slow, but splendid for a man of small means to start farming with, as they are not so expensive and do not require so many oats as horses. Gasoline and steam engines do very quick work. I have seen a gasoline engine pull five ploughs, three disks and a harrow, while a steam engine has seven or eight ploughs.

We have a fine class of settlers here. A great many Americans and Eastern people, not very many French, and a few English. Land costs from twenty to twenty-five dollars an acre. We own a half section, three hundred and twenty acres.

This is a beautiful country, as there are so many pretty wildflowers and beautiful song-birds. In the early morning, about half-past five or six it is just simply grand to hear the birds sing. I often think of what a treat we missed when we lived in town, as we have been on the farm for three years. Two and a half miles north of us is the town of Denholm. The mainline of the C.N.R. runs through Denholm. Eight miles south-east of us is one of the oldest towns in Saskatchewan, Battleford. The Mounted Police Barracks and the Government Indian Schools are located there. Then three miles from Battleford lies the town of North Battleford. It is a railway centre, and at the present time you can hardly get a bed for love or money, as there are so many immigrants coming into the country. Two and a half miles south of us lies the great Saskatchewan river. Then in the background are the beautiful Eagle Hills. They are covered with poplars, birch, evergreens, and are dotted here and there with houses, which make it very pleasant to look upon.

Our school is one mile south from our place. Denholm school is two and a half miles north. Harringay four miles east of us, and Rosecliffe five miles west of us, so you see there are plenty of schools. Perhaps I have made my letter a little long, but there are so many requests for a description of the West, I thought it might be interesting.

Irene Rose

Denholm, Sask.
Family Herald and Weekly Star
June 21, 1919

A Cold Dip

Dear Pathfinders:

Daddy takes the daily Free Press and I see that in the Saturday's paper you have a page for boys and girls. I would like to see my letter in print.

Have any of the Pathfinders lost any cattle with this disease that is going around the country? We lost five. It is called "Hemmorrhagic Septicemia." Three or four of our neighbours lost some cattle. We heard of one man who lost twenty.

We have got the whooping cough now; there are six of us, but my youngest sister has got it the worst. I am pretty well over it.

My brother and I attend a consolidated school. The vans have not been running for three weeks now on account of the roads being so bad, but we hope to start back again on Monday.

A ravine runs just below our house and there is still some snow and ice in it. My brother Geoffrey and I were going to cross it; I stepped on a piece of ice and went up to my waist in the water. My! it was cold. I got out of there quicker than I went in. Geoffrey stood laughing at me and told me to go to the house to change my clothes.

Renne Pettinger (12)

Free Press Prairie Farmer
May 26, 1920

Herding Sheep and Cattle

Dear Pathfinders:

This is my fourth letter to the club. I was going to school in the winter time, but I am not going now because I am herding sheep and cattle. There are 150 cattle and 350 sheep that I am herding. My brother and sister are going to school now. When I left school I was in grade five.

Wallace Williams (10)

Oak Lake, Man.
Free Press Prairie Farmer
July 7, 1920

Plate 25. Saturday bath in the horse's water trough, no date (Martha Knapp Collection, Coll. 146, Provincial Archives of Manitoba [N17468]).

Plate 26. Children with a child's coffin, ca. 1914 (Foote Collection, 183, Provincial Archives of Manitoba [N1783]).

"A Story That Is a Little Tragic"

Drama, Trauma, and Childhood Adventures

Life in rural areas could be difficult if not tenuous, yet children appeared to accept accidents, illness, adventures, and misadventures as a normal part of life. Children experienced nature at its worst in cyclones, blizzards, prairie and forest fires, and at its best during their rambles across fields, through woods, and along streams or seashore. They also witnessed and recorded events that are now part of history. As health professionals were few in number and health care services and facilities often hours if not days away, parents treated injuries and sickness as best they could with patent medicines or materials from their pantries or gardens. But lack of proper treatment left some children with permanently debilitating injuries and lingering effects from illness.

Almost a Shipwreck

Dear Maple Leaves:

Although I did not see my last letter in print I thought I would try again.

I must tell you of a little incident that happened to me several years ago. One day my sister and a neighbor's child and I took a trip to Wallaceburg on the ferry, Conger. Wallaceburg is a little town situated on the River Sydenham. To get to it the boat must sail fourteen miles down the St. Clair until it reaches the mouth of the Syne Carte River, which branches into the Sydenham. We had a fine trip, and everything went well until we reached the St. Clair River on our return journey. We had barely entered the St. Clair when a cry went up that the boat was sinking. The life preservers were pulled down and grabbed by the passengers. The whole boat was in a panic. On the top deck one woman had no less that five life preservers on. In other places men were snatching them away from women and children. The captain immediately headed for Port Lambton where we were landed. It was said that if the boat had been twenty minutes longer on the river she would have sunk with all on board. We remained at Port Lambton for over two hours until the Detroit boat arrived to take us home.

I would like to correspond with members in Newfoundland.

Algernon

A.D. McMurtie
Sarnia, Ont.
Family Herald and Weekly Star
December 6, 1911

Fence Making

Dear Dixie Patton:

About three years ago my father and my brother and myself were taking some wire off a fence. The fence was down the hill from the house.

We used one horse to bring the wire up the hill. Father had all the wire off the posts ready to bring up the hill. My brother and I were getting the wire fastened on the singletree, and I was holding the horse by the head. Just as he got the wire fastened on, the horse went ahead. The wire moved and as it moved it made a lot of noise. The horse thought there was something after her. She knocked me down and went as fast as she could up the hill. The barbed wire caught hold of my clothes. The wire turned me around and around so fast that I could not see where I was going. At last I came to a hollow and as I was going out of the hollow I went to one side. Then the wire could not get at me. After a while I got up and went to the house. I did not feel very well after rolling around as fast as I did.

My coat was torn in a lot of places and my pants were torn, too. The barbs had scratched my legs. My mother thought I was killed at first when she saw me lying half way up the hill. After a while I went out to look for my toque. First I went out to the stable, then I saw the wire going into the stable, so I went into the stable and I saw the horse in her stall. I found my toque fastened on the wire. Then I took the toque off the wire and went into the house. The horse was frightened of wire ever after.

A. Maynard Metcalfe (11)

Grain Growers' Guide
June 10, 1914

The Lightning Falls

Dear Maple Leaves:

I live on a farm about two miles from a town which has about 3,500 in population. I think all boys and girls should have an education, the more the better. Now Leaves, don't you all agree with me there?

We had a little excitement in the summer with lightning. One very hot Sunday, heavy black clouds could be seen rolling up from the east and in a few minutes we were in the midst of a fierce thunderstorm. After about half an hour the storm subsided and as I happened to be looking in the direction of the outbuildings, a little tongue of flame appeared in the peak of the roof, and then directly following it, the whole barn burst into flames from top to bottom. The crop being all in just one day before helped to feed the flames and increase the blaze which lasted for about an hour and a half, gradually smouldering away.

I would like to hear from anyone of the Leaves of either sex (13). Address first to Editor.

Droffil C

Perth, Ont.
Family Herald and Weekly Star
January 7, 1914

My Adventure: A True Story

Well, to begin with I have four sisters, but only one of them is married, and her husband last winter was going to help my brother haul grain, which took about a week's time.

And as my sister is afraid to stay alone I was supposed to keep her company, so I saddled my pony and started on my journey, which was a six mile trip. But I wasn't there two days when she took sick and wasn't able to do the work, so she told me to go home and tell somebody else to come over that was more able to work than myself. So at two o'clock in the afternoon I started, it was warm and sunny so I didn't dress warm, but alas when I got about half way home a blizzard started in the north and as I had to travel north it really was a very unpleasant journey, as my pony couldn't keep the trail, because the wind blew the blinding snow into drifts along the road, and he didn't want to face the storm either. So I got off and walked, thinking that I could possibly find the trail that way, but the drifts were too deep so I couldn't walk either and lost the trail.

Then a sudden terror seized me, that now I'd have to stay on the wide lone prairie and freeze to death. My teeth started to shake in my mouth at the very thought, but I was in luck. I heard a cowboy driving some cattle a little distance off and so I rode towards the sound and soon caught up to the herder and told him I was lost. He asked me to come with him and I did, because I was pretty well chilled. My hands were so numb that I could hardly hold the reins and my feet were so cold that I could hardly keep them in the stirrups. Altho he said it was only a short distance to his house, it seemed a great distance to me: but at last we got there and he let me go in the house while he himself put the horses away. When I stepped into the house a smiling young woman greeted me with a hot fire, which tasted as good to me as a stolen chicken to a hungry coyote.

When I was well warmed, the lady treated me to an apple and orange, and when I found enough courage to speak I told her what I was going home for, so she called one of the men and told him to take me home. He said he would and went for the horses. Before we started she gave me a good hot cup of coffee, which tasted very good and freshened me up a bit, so I was ready to start again. On the way home the fellow asked if I knew at which ranch I had been. I said no, because I didn't, and he told me, and just think the ranch I had always longed to see.

It was two o'clock when I started, but it was seven o'clock when I got home. The next day I took sick and had to lie in bed with a cold and a frozen chin.

Edwin Beingessner (11)

Champion, Alta.
Grain Growers' Guide
March 11, 1914
You forgot to get your story certified or it might have won a prize. DIXIE.

A Long Search

Dear Maple Leaves:

One evening I turned several quick summersaults on the side of a hill—then landed on my head and studied astronomy for a few minutes—with the result that I have plenty of time now for writing, as I am lying flat on my back. I don't want any pity, Leaves, for I have a good time here, with my sister to look after me.

One day last fall my sister and I set out in the morning to hunt for some missing cows. We searched the lake shores all morning for tracks, but our search was fruitless. After dinner we set out again and traversed several miles of bush carefully, landing back at our barn. Again we set out, and after we had walked five miles I heard a faint tinkle of a bell; but this time is was pretty late in the day, but we had determined to bring the cattle home; so we plunged into the swamp below us. After going through the swamp and about a mile over burnt land, from a hill I espied the cows. I hurried on, and we turned them towards home; but they baffled us, and made back about two miles into bush we had never been in. We were several miles from home when the sun set, as I commenced to shout, hoping my dog or Daddy would come. Dad didn't hear, but the dog did, and came to us in the bush. With his help we drove the cows into the barnyard a few hours later.

I would like to hear from some steady Protestant boys over sixteen if they will write first, and I can promise interesting replies.

Girl Guide

Killaloe Sta., Ont.
Family Herald and Weekly Star
March 18, 1914

A Waspy Adventure

One day I went into the woods to pick raspberries. It was a fine cloudless day and I had prospects of getting a nice lot. I found the berry patch and was soon busy. The berries tasted fine. I had nearly filled my pail when I saw a better patch further on. So I climbed over a log to get to it when I heard a buzzing around me and felt something biting me. I ran out of the woods and hurried home. I found a wasp in my pail, so I knew that I had been stung by wasps. I was stung in five places on my arms and legs and they certainly did hurt. I hope I will be entitled to a button.

Margaret Eggleston (14)

Grain Growers' Guide
April 22, 1914

The New Gas Well

The little town of Viking is becoming popular, with the new gas well that was struck a few months ago. They started drilling this well early in the spring. They struck a small flow of gas in the latter part of October, but they did not have enough for Edmonton and Viking. The depth was 2,076. So they decided to dig about 500 feet more. They kept on drilling. On November 4, at 3 o'clock a.m., they struck a flow at a depth of 2,340 feet.

On Saturday, November 7 there was a special train came to Viking with some of the Edmonton people, who came to celebrate the discovery of gas. The roaring of the gas could be heard for six miles. Mr. Martin, who is an Edmonton man, said that they will have plenty of gas, because they want to furnish Edmonton with heat and light. The gas that was let out of the well before a cap could be got to shut off was equal to 720 tons of coal a day.

Sophia Tymich (10)

Viking, Alta.
Grain Growers' Guide
March 24, 1915

Ask for Shower

Dear Editor:

I am twelve years old and would like to belong to your club. I have infantile paralysis and have not walked for nearly four years. I cannot go to school and find it very hard sometimes to find amusement. I would like very much to have a postal shower.

I hope to see my letter in print.

Margaret Wintemule

Sherklan, Ont.
Family Herald and Weekly Star
October 14, 1914

The Prairie Cyclone

It was a sultry day in July, 1909, that my friend and I started from our sod shack for a neighbor's house three miles distant. These people kept the post office, and we were going to get the mail. We had no horse, so we had to walk all the way, and the mosquitoes followed us in clouds.

It was noon when we got there, so we stayed to dinner. We were sitting in the parlor after the meal was over when my friend, looking out the window, saw a funnel-shaped cloud in the west. She said we had better wait and see what happened, for she guessed a storm was coming.

In about five minutes' time the windows began to rattle and the dirt flew in all directions. Boxes, boards, and air, whirled around two or three times and set down, maybe in a wheat field half a mile away.

About four o'clock, when the storm was over, one of the neighbors was so kind as to drive us home. When we got home we found the big teepee of wood blown over. Going into the shack we found half the roof gone, and all the clothing was down in the dirt.

My troubles were greater than anybody's, I thought, as my doll was broken and disabled forever. The men soon had the roof on again, but I have never seen a worse storm since.

Florence Fair

Macklin, Sask.
Grain Growers' Guide
April 22, 1914

A Hail Storm

I wish to tell you about a hail storm that happened last night. In the afternoon it was very hot. There was no wind. About suppertime we saw clouds in the west. The storm started with wind and rain, then the hail came very fast. It soon broke in the windows and the lights went out. We held the bed covers up to the windows. We heard a great noise for a long time. After the storm was over father took the lantern and went and looked at the grain and he found it was destroyed. When he came back we went to look for the turkeys. We had luck in finding them.

Stanley Westin (8)

Youngstown, Alta.
Grain Growers' Guide
August 16, 1916

A Trip to the Coal Mine

My brother said to me one night, "Let us go to the coal mine tomorrow." Then I replied, "All right, we will go." So in the morning at 3 a.m. he came to the house and called. I got ready then we started. We both went to sleep on the way and all of a sudden I heard my brother holler. I jumped up quick to see what was the matter. The horses has turned around and likely would have gone back home, but they had run up against a fence and that stopped them. Then we sat up and talked the rest of the way. When we were going down a big hill alongside of the river one of the horses gave an awful jump and we heard the water splash. We didn't know what frightened her, but as we got down the river we looked back and saw a beaver swimming down the river, so I guess that is what frightened her.

When we got down where we were to dig our coal we unhooked the horses and tied them to the wagon and fed them. Then we took our sacks, pick and shovel up to the seam of coal. It was quite a steep hill we had to climb up. At last we got up there, then my brother picked the coal loose and I picked it up and put it in sacks. When we had five sacks filled I would run and get one of the horses and hitch him to a stone-boat while my brother pulled the sacks down the hill and put them on the boat and he would hold them while I led the horse out to the wagon. We could not drive over the road to the coal because the wagon would upset. We hauled twenty sacks out and thought that would be enough so then we ate our dinner, watered the horses and started back. As we were going down a big hill we broke the neckyoke and we had to tie them up with the tie strap. We looked for the beaver, but it was not there to frighten our horses again. We arrived home none the worse for our adventure and to think we saw a beaver, the first we ever saw.

Lora J. Bearss (14)

Rose Glen, Alta.
Grain Growers' Guide
January 12, 1916

An Event of Yesterday

There is one event in my life which I shall never forget and it seems to me as tho it was only yesterday when it happened, altho it is at least six years ago.

When we first came to Canada from New Zealand we lived at Birtle, Manitoba, for two years, and while we were there my uncle came out from Ireland and lived with us. Then my parents, my only sister and I came to Welwyn, Saskatchewan to live. The distance between Welwyn and Birtle is only about thirty miles, and we took our goods over in a sleigh, uncle doing this while father was working at home. One day uncle went for a load of furniture and as he had not returned by dark we did not think he would come home that night. During the day a strange man came to our house and after walking up and down behind our bush for a long time he came to the house and asked if he could stay all night. Mother said he might and as we did not have many beds she made a small one down stairs. This man had a gun and a watch that he seemed to keep very close to him. When he went to bed he left his gun by the door and his watch on the table. Soon we all retired.

During the night father woke up and on hearing a noise downstairs he woke mother. When we heard the noise we two children awoke. When father had listened for a minute he got up. Mother and he thought it was the man downstairs and he was going to do some mischief. They heard a man go over to the table and pick up the watch. Then he went over and picked up the gun and as we listened we heard him coming upstairs. Father went to the head of the stairs with mother close behind and prepared to knock the man downstairs when he came up. The man struck a match about half way up, but it went out so quickly that father did not see who it was. The man came on up and father was just going to spring on him when he lit another match and they saw it was uncle. Before this father had not been frightened, but now he was to think of what might have been. I have not had such a fright since.

Florence Macgibney (13)

Welwyn, Sask.
Grain Growers' Guide
January 19, 1916

A Runaway

It is about two years since papa and mamma and my little brother and I were going to town early in the spring in the wagon. The horses were used to the sleigh in the winter. We were all in except papa and he was going to get in when the horses started to run. Papa was holding the lines and they broke. Then he had to let them go, and they ran up to a straw stack in the corner of the fence where there was room enough for one horse to go thru, and they ran through it anyway, and upset and we all three fell out under the fence. Mamma and I were hurt, but my little brother flew over the fence in the scrub, so he was not hurt. The horses ran from the straw stack and ran into a bush and there they stopped.

Then I went home and so did mamma, but papa went after the horses and unhitched them and put them in the barn. This was the first runaway I ever had.

Rose B. Hendrick (12)

Millwood, Man.
Grain Growers' Guide
March 1, 1916

A Prairie Fire

Last spring we had a bad prairie fire. My mother was driving up to school for me. I live three and a quarter miles from school. My mother got half a mile from home when all at once she smelt smoke. She looked back and saw the fire and was pretty badly frightened. I had started to walk and got about a mile when I met my mother. We were going on to see if we could get past the fire before it got to the trail but it beat us. Then we saw a man running to fight the fire. We turned to meet him. He wanted a match to back fire it but we had none. We had to stop at a place up west all night. It burnt a stack of our hay and came within a rod of our own barn. My father had a hard time to keep it from the barn. It burnt ten miles or more, and lasted two days and one night. I learned to ride horseback afterwards and rode to school all last summer.

Stephen F. Stratton

Clearfield, Sask.
Grain Growers' Guide
May 19, 1916

A Bush Fire

I shall tell you of an event that took place last summer.

We were in the Timiskaming District spending our summer holidays when it was decided that the whole family and a few friends should go to the falls for a picnic. When we got up the next morning the time seemed to go very slowly and it seemed as if we would never get ready, until finally we were all ready to go.

We all wore old hats and dresses and of all the old things they were the oldest. You would have laughed to see the old hats we had on.

We drove about two miles out and walked quite a distance through the bush, following a trail until we reached the falls. There we were supposed to meet some friends, but as they did not come we ate a very small lunch and went to see what was the matter, their house not being far away.

When we got there we saw the bush just behind their house was burning, people were out fighting the fire and didn't have any time to go to picnics. We decided then to go home at once as things looked pretty smoky and the fire was spreading rapidly, so we started off.

All was pretty safe, until we reached a certain point. There in front of us we saw trees tumbling, the flames shooting upward and the smoke pouring out. The only thing to do was to wet our handkerchiefs and tie them round our noses and run. And we did run, only stopping now and then to rest, until at last we got home.

I think it would be nice if some of the leaves, when writing, would tell of their adventures. I am sure that they would interest others.

Mad March Hare (12)

Jennie Wideman
Guelph. Ont.
Family Herald and Weekly Star
June 23, 1915

A Terrible Storm

I am going to tell you a little story which is a little tragic. When I was a little girl six years of age my father used to drive us to school in the sleigh every morning and night, but as he had to load a car of grain this day, I, along with my elder brother and sister, had to walk to school and unfortunately for me it happened to be blowing and snowing with a temperature of thirty-two below zero. On returning home at night and being the youngest of three I had to lag behind and was almost overcome by the storm. My eldest brother came back to look for me. When he found me he told me my face, ears, nose and knees were frozen, so he rubbed them with snow and I marched on the best I could, but my legs and knees began to ache and when I got home my mother found my nose, ears, knees, and face badly frozen. I was crying, but mother rubbed the frozen parts with snow and coal oil and put me to bed with a poultice of gunpowder on the frozen parts. I was all right in a few days, but I shall remember the time when my little heart was panting coming along the road in the snowdrift from school the rest of my life.

Jessie Graham (11)

Dry River, Man.
Grain Growers' Guide
April 26, 1916

My Unlucky Day

It happened three years ago last summer when we had been away all day. It had rained when we were away, so when I got home I took off my boots and stockings and went barefoot.

My sister Merna said that she was going out to the straw stack, so I said that I would go with her. When we got out there I thought I would run around it, but when I got half way around I stepped on a pitch fork which was lying on the ground. I ran a little piece further, dragging the fork with me. I sat down and jerked it out, and started to scream.

I could not walk, so father carried me to the house which was about twenty rods. I could not sleep all night for the pain. Father got up in the middle of the night and put a poultice on it. I was in bed for about a week because I could not walk, and when I did get up I had to walk on tip-toe.

Eileen Elliot (11)

Arden, Man.
Grain Growers' Guide
June 7, 1916

Saw Parliament Building Burn

Dear Maple Leaves:

I used to live about five miles from the city of Ottawa. We could see the Parliament Buildings, also the Chateau Laurier. We could see two (2) miles of lights. We saw the Parliament Buildings burn. Where I live now you can see the rays of Hamilton city, which is eighteen miles distant.

My eldest brother works the farm, my dad died lately.

We have formed a club at our school, we call it the "Khaki Nine Club." We knit socks for soldiers. If anyone cares to write to me, I will answer at once. I am fourteen (14) years old.

Jolly Girl

Velma Langford
York, Ont.
Family Herald and Weekly Star
January 30, 1918

Healing Powder

Dear Pathfinders:

I am going to tell you about an accident I had when I was five years old. When we first came out to Saskatchewan we lived in a little house and afterward father build a new one. My brothers and sisters and I always played in it before it was finished. One day father made a fence between the old house and the new one and I, forgetting about it, was going to run into the house and ran against it. I cut my face so badly that my whole face was covered with blood. When mother saw me she almost fainted, she thought I had put out my eye. She took me in and washed off the blood and grandmother gave her some healing powder which she put on and bandaged it. She kept putting on the powder and it was healed in eight days and you can still see the mark.

I would like some of you to write to me.

Mary Huber (14)

Lipton, Sask.
Free Press Prairie Farmer
January 22, 1919

Medicine Men

Dear Editor:

You said to write again so here I am. You made a mistake in printing my other letter. I live 65 miles from our post office and white neighbors, not five as you printed. Seven Pathfinders wrote to me. Nearly all the Indians are away now trapping in the bush. One day in summer a moose swam across the river by our house, and one day last spring a deer ran across on the ice. Nearly every day I go for walks in the woods and often see tracks of fur animals. We have only seen one white person since last summer. I go to visit the old Indian people quite a lot. I have lived here four years and at Norway House two years before that. We have a rowboat as all our travelling in summer must be by boat and in winter by dog team. This country is rivers, lakes and muskegs. Seven old conjurors or medicine men live here. Some of the people are afraid of them but I am not. Our Indians live by trapping in winter and fishing in summer. They are Saultaux Indians.

Albert Lee (9)

Poplar River Mission
Berens River, Man.
Free Press Prairie Farmer
March 19, 1919

An Indian Doctor

Dear Pathfinders:

This time I am going to tell you how an Indian saved my grandfather's leg from being amputated. When I saw Alfred Beren's letter it made me think of it. Of course, I was not there, but I'm telling it the way my father told me.

Grandpa was out cutting timber with another man, when the other fellow's axe slipped and went into grandpa's thigh. He was taken home and the doctors were called and they [said] the leg would have to be amputated, but grandpa said no. Just then an old Indian came in and looked at him and said, "Me fix," and away he went to the bush. In about half an hour he was back with an armful of roots of all kinds and a pot of muck. He then boiled the roots and made a poultice of them. He put the muck on to keep the steam in, and away he went till morning. Very soon the pain left and grandpa could sleep. The Indian kept applying fresh roots for some days. Grandpa got better and was not even lame. But the Indian would not take any money. I saw Merry Person's letter about pulling nails with old shoes and lifters. Boys would not be so foolish as to waste time with an old shoe; they get a hammer and have it out. And you think that boys are only good for outside work. I don't think. As for myself I can knit, work button holes, makes (sic) French knots, and hemstitch, and darn two ways, one way like real knitting. I can sew with a machine and know what all the attachments are for and am starting to take music lessons now. I, like the rest of you, am a book-worm. I have a dog that will stop and start as soon as far as he can hear me shout. I made harness for him. I made it exactly like Eaton's pioneer set, only with a breast collar. I made a little stone boat, too.

George Hayes (13)

Valley Centre, Sask.
Free Press Prairie Farmer
April 2, 1919

Brownie Chases Me

On February 9, 1914, I upset a pot of water on my foot. It was boiling hot. One week later I went to stay at a nurse's home, living on a farm, six miles north of our house. Her name was Mrs. Young.

A few weeks later one of her cows calved. It was a wild one, and about a week later I was going down to the stable when the cow saw me. What with running and her head lowered, she looked as if she meant business.

I was very much frightened, but could not run, because my foot was scalded. Faster and faster came the cow. I tried to hop on the other one till I reached the wheat granary. There was a box in front of the door, so I just leaned over and went in head first. They said afterward all that could be seen was a rubber and a sugar bag.

Olive Woodward (14)

North Battleford
Grain Growers' Guide
February (n.d.)

Lost in the Bush

Dear Pathfinders:

I would like to tell you how I was once lost at the Red Deer River.

One day my father and mother and myself went to get a load of brush. We had a team of oxen. When we got there, my father and I went to give the oxen a drink at the river, which was a good distance away. We came to a small piece of water on the way, and father let the oxen stay there, and told me to stay with them until he came back, as he was going to the river to get drinking water. Just after he had gone the oxen started back and instead of keeping to the trail, they went right through the bush, and the flies were bad. I could not get through so I started on the trail, which was the wrong way. I walked all day, and could not see anything but bush. It began to get dark, and I could not find any way out of it. I looked around and found a nice place to sleep, and it began to lightning and thunder, and I was asleep and slept a long time. My, I was scared. When I woke up it was light, and I walked on again. I found my way out and started for a house when I heard a man calling me. He had two barrels of water, and I was so thirsty I thought I could drink it all. He took me to his house and gave me something to eat. I was nearly two days and a night without anything to eat or drink, and six miles from where I got lost. I lost my hat and a boot and got my foot full of cactus pricks. I was only four years old, and that was in 1914, and so you can guess it was no joke. I don't think so. I will be very pleased to hear from any Pathfinders, and will answer all letters.

Stanley W. Cox (8)

Vandyne, Alta.
Free Press Prairie Farmer
April 2, 1919

Escaped Bandits

Dear Pathfinders:

This is my birthday and I am 11 years of age, and am going into Grade VIII in three weeks.

I live in the Rockies, and the mountains are beautiful with wild flowers. The Old Man River runs through here. There is a cave in the mountains near Crow's Nest, where the water comes rushing out and it is called the source of the Old Man River.

There had been great excitement over the train robbery. The bandit who escaped when one bandit and two policemen were killed was caught yesterday.

About 100 policemen were here and were searching the mountains day and night. It is a very difficult task, as there is so much bush. One of the bandits is still at large.

John Lloyd

Free Press Prairie Farmer
September 8, 1920

Plate 27. Saluting the flag, undated, but possibly ca. World War I (BC Archives [24812]).

Plate 28. Eighteen-year-old Pte. Jack Craig of Winnipeg posed with his parents and three of his siblings before leaving for Europe. The photo was taken May 17, 1915, and he was killed in action in Ypres, France, June 12, 1916 (photograph in the collection of Norah Lewis).

"My Father Has Enlisted"
Children and the First World War

Although Canadian and Newfoundland children were far from the war zone, war touched and shaped their lives and their attitudes. In 1914, they, like many adults, were swept up in the patriotic fervour of the time. They were anxious to do their part and ready to sacrifice time and energy, if not their very lives, for king and country. They were appalled and saddened when the human toll of war touched their families and communities. They rejoiced when the "war to end all wars" was over and they hoped peace would endure forever.

Explains the War

Dear Maple Leaves:

Maurine, an Ontario girl, asks if any of the Leaves can tell her the cause of the present European War. The quarrel began by the murder of the Crown Prince of Austria and his wife, by a Servin. For this horrid outrage, the Austrian government made certain demands on the Servin government. Servia yielded to most of these demands, and what she could not agree to, she wished to settle by arbitration. This did not satisfy Austria, so Austria declared war on Servia.

The European nations are like a band of warriors who live together as neighbors, but do not agree very well. Some are big and strong, others are small and weak. When any trouble arises the big powers generally take a large share in it and help to decide the matter. The parties on either side are pretty equally divided, and this often makes it difficult to prevent a war.

A war between Austria and Servia was like a fight between a strong man and a small boy, and Russia being related to Servia, would not stand aside to allow Servia to be crushed. When Russia began to collect her troops to warn Austria to be cautious, Germany sent word to Russia that unless she stopped these war preparations within twelve hours Germany would declare war on Russia. Russia had no intention of making war so long as there was hope of a peaceful settlement. France, Britain, and Italy tried to get the other powers to work together for peace, but before anything could be done, Germany declared war against Russia, and at the same time, Germany set out to attack France, because France had agreed to help Russia if war broke out.

Now Germany had planned to attack France by sending soldiers through Belgium in order to attack France at her weakest part. This was breaking the law of nations and the Belgians would not allow it without a fight. It was also breaking a treaty with Britain, which declared that neither France nor Germany should be allowed to attack each other by sending troops through Belgium. So Belgium and Britain were drawn into the struggle against Germany.

Some years ago France took all her warships away from the coasts that lie near Britain. This relieved the British from fear of attack by France and showed the British that the French trusted them, so when war broke out, Britain felt obliged to defend these coasts against German attack. So Russia is helping Servia against

Austria and is also at war with Germany. France entered the war to help Russia. Belgium is fighting against an unprovoked invasion by Germany, and Britain is helping France and Belgium.

The German Government would not take part in helping to arrange for a peaceful settlement when the quarrel began between Austria and Servia. They seem to have wanted a war to get a chance to rule all western Europe, by driving as the Boers would say, the Danes, the Dutch, the Belgians and the French into the sea and making these countries states of the German Empire. This would soon cause the downfall of Britain also. Then Austria would like to rule the Balkan States, but Russia cannot allow this.

Germany's ambition is to build an empire greater than any the world has yet known. This is what her great armies and navies are for. It is hoped that the European War may show that it is better to build an empire on justice, freedom and brotherhood, rather than on armaments.

Farm Boy

Sask.
Family Herald and Weekly Star
October 28, 1914

Canada and the War

When England was forced to take a place in this great war she appealed to her colonies for help. The loyality of the Canadians was shown by the immediate enlistment of their bravest men. This event took place in August 1914, and up to the present time Canada has answered the repeated call for recruits.

Canada is assisting the allies financially as well as in other ways, through the Daughters of the Empire, Red Cross societies, Patriotic, and Belgium Relief Funds. These great societies are sewing and knitting for our soldiers and are raising money in different ways to buy necessities for them. Large contributions have been sent to the allies' starving women and children.

Although the war has caused much sorrow and suffering it has been a a benefit in some ways. Since we cannot purchase goods from foreign countries, we are learning to manufacture them ourselves.

After the war we expect that there will be a great immigration. Many who have lost their lands and homes in this war will be glad to come out and live in a free country. There will be many invalided soldiers to be looked after. As most of our ablest men have enlisted it will take time before we shall have as brave and strong a type of man as we had before this great crisis occurred.

I am enclosing a picture of myself on my horse, Nellie. Wishing the club success.

Phyllis F. Collins (10)

Saltcoats, Sask.
Free Press Prairie Farmer
January 30, 1918

My Opinion on War

These days all eyes are turned on the great war now raging in Europe. Tho we do not actually see it, we know enough of its horrors and sufferings to make us realize how terrible war really is.

Now war in general is a thing that should not exist. How dreadful it is to think of nations calling themselves civilized, who have to clash together in arms, because they are simply not able in peace to settle questions concerning their honor, the result being that hundreds of thousands of men in the prime of life are killed like beasts and many more are mortally wounded. Then to think of all the sorrow in the homes where a father or a husband had heard the call to duty, gone to the battlefield, never to return again, makes many regret that war had ever existed.

These are some reasons why I think war does more harm than good. In time of war there are usually thousands of people who have to starve for want of food as in the case of some of the countries in this conflict. Also after a war which has lasted a long period one side is usually financially gone, and it takes many years to come back to its former standard. And last, but not least, is the regret which will continue for years to come among the nations who are to blame for such terrible war.

Never will the world be what it should be until war is forever stopped, and men of every nationality live together like brothers.

Heidmar B. Bjornson (14)

Vidar, Man.
Grain Growers' Guide
June 21, 1916

War
(A Prize Story)

I think war is a curse to the world. After every war there is always a few years of hard times, the country is weakened on account of nearly all her young and able-bodied men being killed. The country is neglected and does not produce the crops it should and there is therefore a scarcity of home-grown foods, which causes the cost of living to go up. Millions of dollars worth of metal goes to the bottom of the sea, and when it is all over what better off is the nation? It is worse, it is poorer, weaker, and the countries that have been invaded are left a mass of wreck and ruin. For, example, look at Belgium, which before this war was the foremost country in agriculture, now being overgrown with weeds. What once were fertile fields are being dug up to form trenches. In England and Scotland men holding large estates are being so heavily taxed they will, if this war lasts much longer, have paid more that the value of the land. For years Germany has been robbing her people by levying large taxes to prepare for this war, and now she is borrowing all her people's gold and silver and giving them paper instead. The gold and silver is going out of the country and when the war is finished, when the people present their paper to receive the money where is it to come from when it is not in the country?

John Wilson (13)

Milnerton, Alta.
Grain Growers' Guide
June 21, 1916

In Canadian Forestry Battalion

Dear Ex-Members:

I have been reading your interesting letters, and being lonesome today, I am going to write a few lines.

I belong to the 224th Forestry Battalion, and went to Bramshot last May. We drilled for a few weeks there, and then came up to Scotland to work in the woods where we are now, at least some of us, as the Battalion is now spread over Great Britain and France in camps.

The chief trees are Scotch fir and larch. The fir resembles the Norwegian pine, and some of it is very large. We have a saw-mill and make most of the timber into railway ties for the front, besides boards and deal.

The winter here is a new thing to me, as we only had a little frost and snow; the sky is cloudy most of the time. This sounds strange, as I am used to the frost of New Brunswick.

The logs are hauled over poleroads by horses and the ties are taken to the stations by steam tractors, and then taken to the coast for shipment.

Our camp is seven miles from Nairn, the nearest town, so we are pretty well back in the woods. Forres, another nearby town, is Lord Strathcona's birthplace.

Should any members care to write to a boy of nineteen, I would answer all letters. I should like to hear from Gipsy Love as I hope to go the wilds of British Columbia should I get back, and would like information about that country. We have a good many men from British Columbia with us.

                                            Lumber Jack

Scotland
Family Herald and Weekly Star
May 9, 1917

Christmas in the Trenches

Dear Ex-Leaves:

As this Christmas has not been the same to me as all my other Christmas Days I thought I would like you to know how a soldier in France spent his Christmas Day, and also Christmas Eve.

Twas the day before Christmas when I returned to my battalion from the Division School, where I was taking a course in bombing,—though I am a trained bomber I can always learn more. We had dinner, consisting of beans, bread, and tea at 12:30 o'clock. At one o'clock we were to leave for the trenches, with "heavy marching order," about eight miles.

At one o'clock sharp,—about twenty of them (the rest of the battalion was already in the trenches) fell in and marched off. Four o'clock found us just turning on the trench mats which led into the trenches across the country, an hour and a half later found us sitting on the road just where we enter the communication trench that leads to the front line.

After a walk of about a half an hour up the trench we came to a trench branching off to the right. One of the boys ran up the trench branching off to the right. One of the boys ran up a trench a little way and met an English soldier, and asked him if he knew where the ___ Battalion was. He told us to go up the trench we were in. "There's some Canadians up there, the Princess Pats, isn't it?" For the boys don't know one battalion from another,—we have to laugh at those chaps.

A little further we met one of the companies of our battalion, and they told us our company had gone out. With the help of a guide who came with us we reached our company in about an hour's time.

By this time the boys were "all in," and were about to give up, and to make it all the worse the dugouts were full. Don't forget we had nothing to eat since noon.

My mate and I walked all over the place looking for a place to sleep, and to get out of the rain which was now falling. At eleven o'clock we had run on to one of our field kitchens where we got some tea in a cigarette case and some biscuits.

As we were walking back from our fine supper I noticed a hole in the ground, and looking more closely we found it was, or had been a dugout, so we went in, and lighted a little bit of a candle which my chum had in his pocket. the water as dropping through in places, and the mud in the bottom was two inches deep but it had to do. We got a few sand bags which were lying in the corner, spread them in the mud, laid our rubber sheet on top, used our packs for pillows, lay down, and put the two blankets, (which we carried), over us with our coats on top, and before we went to sleep my chum said, "Will you ever forget this Christmas Eve?"

At eight o'clock in the morning we poked our heads out from under the wet blankets, looked out to find it raining. For breakfast we got a loaf of bread, to last the two of us all day, and some tea. (The bacon was all finished.)

We went back to the dugout and slept till dinner time. For dinner we got two tablespoonsful of butter, and a tin of jam between five, and some tea. In the afternoon we sat in the dugout and smoked and talked; for supper we had roast beef, bread and tea.

We were warned in the afternoon of "Gas Guard" from six till seven next morning; my shift was from six till eight—nothing happened.

At ten o'clock sharp all the guns around here opened fire, just as if someone had pressed a button: this was still going on when I went on again at twelve o'clock.

Now, Leaves, I am only seventeen and saw some of this when I was sixteen, and know all about it. I am only a mere boy, but I thought I was a man, and now I know I have got to stick to it. I was also in hospital for six weeks. I guess I have said enough. I hope to hear from you girls who send cake to soldier boys doing their "bit" and you soldier boys like myself.

Not a Hero

Pte. J. D. Thomson
No. 709837, No.1, Co'y., 102 Battalion, C.E.F.
London, England
Family Herald and Weekly Star
March 7, 1917
I am very pleased to publish your interesting letter, and hope some "Cake sending girls" will do their "bit." We are very proud of our soldier Leaves.—Editor.

A Sailor in Training

Dear Maple Leaves:

I am now serving as a sailor in the dock yard at Victoria, B.C. I have been in the Navy about two months and think it is a good thing for boys.

The training is not hard, only the cutlass drill which is done with long swords which make your wrists ache: I have not been aboard many ships yet, but I hope to be going aboard some pretty soon.

I would like to correspond with any other Leaves who would like to write first.

A Young Jacktar

A. Vaux, R.N.C.V.R.
Naval Yard, Esquimalt, B.C.
Family Herald and Weekly Star
August 15, 1917

Describes Wounded Soldiers

Dear Maple Leaves:

I have been to see the wounded men that have just returned. There are hundreds of wounded soldiers at the Military Hospital in Witworth Street, so if there are any Manchester readers they will know the place quite well. At the side of the hospital is a small park where the soldiers can take a walk—those few who are able to walk! I saw one poor fellow, nineteen years of age, being wheeled about in a bath chair. He was in the fierce battle at Mons. His right leg was shot away. He was only a lad, but quite manly looking.

There is always a crowd of spectators around the park, but as no one is allowed to go inside, the soldiers come close to the railings. Here they tell us about their experiences on the battlefield. Gifts of fruit, flowers, cigarettes and money are passed through the railings to the soldiers.

There was a Scottish soldier from Glasgow, relating how he came to be shot. I was right near him and heard his story all through. He and his mates were firing from the trenches when a shell exploded right above their heads. Five men near him were killed instantly, while a great number were wounded. The soldier was badly hurt in the back, and he walked only with the greatest difficulty. Another, an English soldier, had half his face shot away. His head and face are bandaged up, all except one eye, so that he could manage to see.

One of the soldiers was in the 9th Lancers. No doubt you have heard of the magnificent charge of the 9th Lancers. He was one of the men who rushed the line, cut the German gunners down, spiked the guns, and then rode back to our lines—but with heavy losses to the British. He is to receive the Victoria Cross for valour.

It was a pitiful sight to see these men. There were only a few who smiled at all, and then they did not smile much.

A friend of mine has gone abroad. His destination is to be kept secret as they are moving under sealed orders. My brother is leaving England for the front next week I expect.

We are so pleased to know that America has given Germany the "cold shoulder." America is beginning to see who is deserving of their sympathy. This is going to be a three years' war.

Last week I saw 50 Belgian refugees arrive here in Manchester. It was pitiful to see them carrying all their belongings in small bundles. Among them was a cat, photographed with the other refugees. As they passed us, we all waved and cheered them and all except one poor boy waved back. He looked too scared. I don't know what he passed through. They had a grand reception in Manchester. They had tea in the Town Hall. I could see them through the windows, and afterwards they were conveyed in motor cars to the different homes provided for them.

If the French would use their new gun oftener, it would be much better. It is so made that when it explodes it suffocates all around it. That would be a far more merciful death than being bayonetted or wounded in any way.

Well, dear Leaves, I will close for now or you will be getting bored. I would like to exchange post cards with Indians. Best wishes to all.

Rose Buerdsell

12 Broughton St.
Cheetham Hill Road
Manchester, England
Family Herald and Weekly Star
November 18, 1914

Wounded Soldiers on Parade

Dear Ex-Leaves:

I think the letters are most interesting, especially from lonely soldiers boys, and it is just a lonely way to get to know friends and exchange words and ideas on different things, don't you think so.

I live in the country, but I prefer city life because it is not a bit lonesome.

I lived in the city of Winnipeg all last fall and winter, and when I was there I saw what I thought a terrible sight—over one thousand returned soldiers on parade, those that were unable to walk were riding in cars provided by the Returned Soldiers' Association of Winnipeg. I have seen them both leaving for the front and coming home maimed and disabled fo life.

I had a cousin who joined up in the early part of the war, but was killed about last October.

How many of you like riding horseback? I think it is great fun.

I like cooking, housework, sewing and crocheting. I also have a great collection of shoulder badges, which I think are nice to keep in rememberance.

If any one cares to write I will try to answer their letter, especially soldier boys.

Lover of Khaki

Family Herald and Weekly Star
October 17, 1917

Father Killed in Action

Dear Maple Leaves:

The weather had been very dry all spring and the last two weeks it has been very cold and frosty.

Our family has had pretty near its share of the war. My father was killed in action in the Passchendale Ridge Battle in November, and my uncle is in France now.

There are six children in our family. Three boys and three girls. My baby brother was born two days before dad left for France and it is hard to believe he will never see him again.

I have a white pony named Babe who is quite a good saddle horse even if she is small.

We have twenty-five head of cattle and sixteen head of horses. Four of the horses are little colts who are as pretty and cute as can be.

Soldier Girl

Evelyn Price
Ewing, Alta.
Family Herald and Weekly Star
June 19, 1918

Leaf from a Mohawk Tribe

Dear Maple Leafs:

I am a little girl, ten years old, and I belong to the Mohawk tribe of the Six Nation Indians. My father has enlisted, and so have many others from this reserve.

I would like to correspond with some other little girl of my age, whose father has enlisted.

Olive Powless

Wilsonville, Ont.
Family Herald and Weekly Star
March 22, 1916

Father and Brother in the Army

Dear Maple Leaves:

I would like very much to join the Maple Leaf Club and to correspond with any of the Leaves, if they will write first. I am alone out here in Canada, and it would cheer me up very much to be able to join the club. I am the youngest of three sons; my two brothers are serving their country. One was wounded in Flanders; the other is in the 19th Dragoons. My father is a doctor in the Indian Army Medical Corp, and my mother is a countess in Italy.

I used to go to grammar school in England and played a great deal of football, and was in the first cricket eleven, but I got ill with appendicitis and that is why I'm out here. Every week I read your letters, Leaves, and they interest me very much and at last I thought I would join your club. I am sixteen and a half years old. Hoping to hear from some of the Leaves.

Francis Ekman

Lone Rock, Sask.
Family Herald and Weekly Star
February 23, 1916

Two "Maple Leaves" in the Office

Dear Maple Leaves:

I would like to be a Leaf on your Tree. I am working in the Evening Telegram Office. I am sixteen years old and have two brothers in the 1st Newfoundland Regiment, one is missing, the other is still at the front. I went to enlist myself, but they would not take me then; but I have not given up hope yet. They are having recruiting parades here at night time, headed by different bands, and they have got a lot of recruits in this way. I do not like to see animals ill-treated. I have five dogs of my own. I would like to correspond with any Leaves and will try to answer all letters. There is another Maple Leaf where I am working, his pen name is Painter's Lackie.

Not a Slacker

H.V. Tuff, c/o Evening Telegram
St John's, Nfld.
Family Herald and Weekly Star
January 10, 1917

Taking Military Training

Dear Maple Leaves:

I hope that I will be admitted into this wonderful club. I have been going to join your ranks for over a year, but I couldn't write a letter that anyway suited me. This one doesn't either, but it has to do.

I live at the junction of the Welland Canal and Lake Erie. The canal goes through the centre of our town, cutting the front streets. They face each other but on opposite sides of the canal.

I am in second form at high school. I love the languages—Latin, French and German—but I am not fond of mathematics.

I suppose the Leaves know "Tipperary." It is very popular here. I am learning to play the piano. I like to play patriotic pieces, and I often amuse myself in the evening by learning new ones.

There are a number of soldiers here guarding the locks, the Government mill and the elevators. Every night after four they train all the boys, the little ones included. We girls asked if we couldn't be trained too, so now we are taking military training. I am very fond of it for I am a regular tomboy. I love racing, jumping fences, skating, etc. I am thirteen years of age, healthy and strong.

Dorothy Boyle

Port Colborne, Ont.
Family Herald and Weekly Star
December 2, 1914

A Cadet Corp

Dear Maple Leaves:

I am going to tell you about our Cadet Corp. It is No. 504 and when we are all present there are about 60 officers and men.

I am a private in the 3rd section. In the spring we have drill once a week. The Government supplies us with suits and rifles. There are 32 Ross rifles for the little ones and rifles the same as the soldiers use for the big boys. I have a large one. After the inspection on the 19th May, before a major, we had a dish of ice cream.

We always go to camp at Kingston for a week in July. But this year The Government would not vote any money, so we have to wait till next year, and we might see the Kaiser. The captain of our corp is in the third contingent, so we have a new one.

I see many Leaves have friends in the war. I have a cousin in France with the 2nd Battalion. A lot of men went from here.

All I wish is to be with the Canadians in France. When I grow up I will either be a sailor or a soldier. I cannot be a bugler for my parents do not want me to.

I would like correspondents in Canada or from foreign countries. I like Leaves from harbors and seaports.

Deerslayer

Andrew Vannaeto
Penly Pool, Ont.
Family Herald and Weekly Star
July 7, 1915

A Visit to a Military Camp

Dear Maple Leaves:

I am a Canadian girl, fourteen years old, and I live on a farm in British Columbia. I like farm life pretty well, but would like it better if it wasn't so quiet. I have one brother who enlisted for overseas service last June. He went first to the military camp at Vernon, and then his battalion was sent to Vancouver. My sister and I went up to see him when he was in Vernon. We had to travel by boat and by train; there were four thousand soldiers in the camp. On Sunday morning we saw the soldiers on Church Parade. They were so well drilled that they marched just as one man.

On Sunday night a company (that is two hundred and fifty men) went away; one of the bands marched them down from the camp to the depot. There was a special train for them because they were going right through to Quebec. A great crowd went to see them off. It took the soldiers about half an hour to march on to the train, and during that the people cheered and the band played patriotic music.

The next day we saw them drilling, some were signalling with flags, while others answered them with the guns. Others went through different kinds of drill. I think Canada ought to be proud of her brave soldiers.

I am fond of music and am learning to play the violin. It is difficult, but very interesting.

I would like to correspond with boys or girls from fourteen to seventeen.

Only a Girl

Lillian Davidson
West Bank, B.C.
Family Herald and Weekly Star
February 16, 1916

The Governor's Visit

Dear Maple Leaves:

This is my second letter to the Maple Leaf Club. I did not see my first letter in print, but I hope I shall see this one. I take a very great interest in your letters.

We had a visit from His Excellency the Governor General and Lady Davidson, on November 1, 1916. They visited all the homes of those whose sons had been killed at the front. The Governor gave a lecture in the Orange Hall and there was a large audience there to greet him.

I have three brothers and two sisters, and all of us attend school. This year I am going for the Primary Examination and my eldest sister the Intermediate. I would like to correspond with any Leaves my own age (11).

Pink Rose

Flossie M. Thompson
Bonavista, Nfld.
Family Herald and Weekly Star
January 31, 1917

Consecration Day in Vancouver

Dear Ex-Leaves:

Perhaps the Leaves will be interested in how Vancouver observed the afternoon of Consecration Day, the anniversary of the day on which Great Britain declared war.

The programme started with a great procession of 5,000 people, and I was one of them. The procession started down in the heart of the city,—there were three bands. There were a great many soldiers, some police and firemen, and the rest were citizens. We marched through the main business streets for over a mile until we reached Cambie street grounds, where the exercises were held. There were 60,000 people packed along the line of the march. We marched four abreast, and the police force kept a narrow path clear, just wide enough for us to pass through. The people were massed on every street for fifteen blocks, and in every building and place they could see from. On the Cambie street grounds a great many speeches were made with the assurance that our country and her Allies will carry the war to a victorious end. The national anthems of Great Britain, France, Russia, Belgium, Italy and Japan were played by the bands and sung by the vast audience. A prayer was made after each anthem. We were lined up in ranks for two hours while the speeches were being made, and after that "Rule Britannia" was sung by the audience. Then we marched out in front of the Drill Hall on Beatty street and here dispersed. It was the greatest demonstration in the history of Vancouver.

British Columbia

Family Herald and Weekly Star
October 6, 1915

Empire Day

Dear Maple Leaves:

I am going to change my pen-name as the Editor had asked me to.

I must tell you how we spent Empire Day at Buffet. First we went to the school and the teacher read to us a lovely book called "King's Call." Then we sang British songs such as "Rule Britannia" and "Soldiers of the King." After that we paraded round the harbor and came back to the playground where we spent the remainder of the time in games, which our teacher Mr. Cliett showed us, and which most of us took an interest in. After games were over, Mrs. Shorter came along, throwing candy, and gave us all some cake which ended our Empire party.

How many of the other Leaves spent Empire Day like that? I would like to hear from any who kept Empire Day, telling me all about it.

Maritime

Annie Upshall
Hr. Buffet, Placentia Bay, Nfld.
Family Herald and Weekly Star
July 21, 1915

A Small Boy's Bit

I'd like to join the army
    And do my little bit,
But as I'm only a youngster
    I guess that I'm not fit.

But I AM fit to stay at home
    And help upon the farm
To feed the pigs, and do the chores,
    Won't do me any harm.

I'll work out in the field this fall
    As hard as ever I can,
Then dad can pat my head and say,
    "You're doing your bit, my man."

I'll save my dimes and nickels
    That I used to spend before,
And I'll send them on to Belgium
    To the needy and the poor.

God help the poor, brave soldiers,
    The lads so brave and true,
We're fighting for our dear old flag,
    The Old Red, White, and Blue.

                              Sterling Dorcas (13)

Therso, Sask.
Free Press Prairie Farmer
February 13, 1918

Thrilling Pictures

Dear Ex-Leaves:

I am writing to wish you all a very happy New Year. I suppose a great many of you have had your skates sharpened up for the great Canadian sport, ice skating. I have had my skates on this season, but unfortunately developed a severe cold which put me out of the skating class for a while. Still staying in the house has its compensations,—I can knit socks for the boys in the trenches.

How many of you have seen the "Battle of the Somme" pictures? They are splendid I can assure you, and enable us to realize better what the brave soldiers are doing. I saw these pictures in Edmonton; the crowds that attended were enormous.

One picture showed British artillery moving up to the front through a field on which were the dead bodies of some of the brave Gordon Highlanders. Another showed British Tommies burying German dead. While these scenes were on the orchestra played "Nearer My God to Thee,"—it was intensely sad many of the audience were wiping their eyes. But there were more cheerful than sad ones. One of these showed British Soldiers receiving mail in the trenches. "Keep the Home Fires Burning' played then. I am sure very few of us realized the part played by these brave men who have the Red Cross on their arms until we saw those pictures showing them attending to the wounded, they were simply great.

Every Leaf who has a soldier relative should try to see those pictures to help them see for themselves the sacrifices the boys make when they leave their homes to fight for King and Country. And the "slackers," well they should be made to see them.

The young people in this district are planning a box social and patriotic concert to be held quite soon. They are going to invite the young people of the surrounding school districts to take part in the programme, and ask every girl to bring a basket or box; in this way we hope to make the affair a success—I will let the Leaves know how it succeeds.

I am knitting all the time for the Red Cross,—we have a circle here. I knitted about sixteen pairs of socks during 1916 and I hope to do better during 1917. The more knitters the better, so girls here's your chance to do your bit.

I would like Union Jack to know that I wrote to him as he invited me to do in his recent letter to the Corner, also Pte. Arnold Smith of the 193 Nova Scotia Highlanders, another Leaf who asked me to write. Farmer Soldier, I will write to you if you will write first.

Eileen Aroon

Alta.
Family Herald and Weekly Star
January 17, 1917

Ten Thousand People Celebrated

Dear Maple Leaves:

We were all pleased on hearing of peace terms here in Sarnia last Monday morning.

We were awakened by the whistle of Port Huron, which set up a racket, the like of which has never been heard.

It took some time to discover what Port Huron was raising all the racket about. It was impossible to get Port Huron either by phone or telegraph.

The Sarnia citizens band was out in strong number and in no time kept the air filled with their stirring selection.

When they played the National Anthem a silence fell over the vast crowd and every head was bared until the music stopped.

The Kilties were there, of course, their music was just as conspicuous as it ever is.

The pipes, drums, tub pans, and old kettles, in fact anything that would make a noise.

Golden Head

Mary Giffel
Sarnia, Ont.
Family Herald and Weekly Star
November 27, 1918

Plate 29. Entrance to the main shaft of the Nanaimo Coal Mine, undated (BC Archives [49564]).

Plate 30. Wash day at Kingcome Inlet, undated (Columbia Coast Collection, The Anglican Synod of British Columbia and the Yukon).

"I Worked in a Pulp-Mill"
Part of the Work Force

By age twelve to fourteen many youngsters were doing adult work and carrying adult responsibilities. Boys frequently followed their fathers' vocations as farmers, fisherman, or railway workers. Girls generally emulated their mothers as homemakers or domestics. Other youngsters however, whether from desire or necessity, left home to join the work force. They played an important role in Canadian agriculture and industry during the war years, 1914-1918. Youngsters who received at least part of their secondary school education or undertook specialized training generally had access to a wider range of vocational opportunities than youngsters who left school with minimal education. Young workers were proud of their ability to work and of their success in the working world.

Near the Age Limit

Dear Maple Leaves:

Here comes a sixteen-year-old bud to join your club. I live on a farm two miles north of Cowley. It contains ninety acres of land, a part of it under cultivation. I have three head of horses of my own, and I have twenty-four acres of fall wheat. I worked all last summer to put it in. Do any of the Leaves like fishing? I catch quite a few fish.

We had lots of skating on the river, but last week there came a big snowstorm and covered all the ice, but we are making a rink. We have lots of shooting here, as there are plenty of jack rabbits. I had a shot gun, but I traded it for a saddle. I have a twenty-two now. I do lots of riding now and I read quite a bit. I would like to correspond with any of the Leaves. Goodbye.

Country Bumpkin

Cowley, Alta.
Family Herald and Weekly Star
March 18, 1914

Worked in Pulp-Mill

Dear Maple Leaves:

I read the Maple Leaf letters every week and enjoy them very much, so I thought I should like to become a member of this memorable club. Just now I am having a little vacation, well earned, too, I think, for I have worked hard all winter. I worked in a pulp-mill and like it very much. I live in the country and a very beautiful place it is. We have some very valuable fishing grounds in this part of the country and tourists come here every summer. Not far from here is the pretty Kejimkujik Lake where the club house and cabins are for summer sports and in my leisure moments I have caught many a speckled beauty.

Some of the boys have queer ideas about the girls. For my part I like girls as a rule, and think the world a pretty poor place to live in were it not for them. I am also in favor of the Suffragettes. Why should they not have the franchise? They are just as capable of voting for the betterment of our country as are the men.

I should like to correspond with Rideau Lassie, who is my own age (14) and Strike Three if they will please write first. I can tell them some interesting stories about pulp-mill work.

In closing, I wish the editor and Leaves all success, and hope to receive my badge very soon.

I am rather puzzled about a name, but I have decided on "Hiawatha," or if any other Leaves chance to have this name will the Editor please give me

"Mudjekeewis"

R.S. Sarty
Harmony Mills, Queen's Co., N.B.
Family Herald and Weekly Star
September 2, 1914

Keeping Post Office

Dear Maple Leaves:

I have an occupation that takes up most of my time. I am postmistress at this place, a small village. I am quite young (16) but understand and take an interest in my work. It is my brother-in-law that has the office. He is postmaster.

Well, Leaves, I suppose you are all thinking of Xmas. I know I am, it will soon be here.

Did any of your Leaves ever go to a dance? I was at one in September and had a lovely time. Dancing is my choice of indoor sports and coasting, skating and sleigh riding are my three chief outdoor sports.

I love to read stories. My favorite author is L.M. Montgomery.

                                      Sweet Sixteen

Louise Audrey Pugh
Buritts's Corner, York Co. N.B.
Family Herald and Weekly Star
October 31, 1917

Telegraph Operator

Dear Maple Leaves:

I am fourteen years old, and live on a farm not far from a pretty village situated on the side of a river.

We have the telegraph office in our home. My two sisters and myself are operators. I go to school also and am in the second model; I am going to study to be a teacher.

I like reading and read the continued story, "The Vanished Messenger." I have also read the Elsie books, most of the Alger books and many others. I have three sisters and three brothers. I would like to correspond with Bleeding Heart, Priscilla, Chatterbox, and any of the Leaves if they would please write first.

Little Tranquillity

Bertha P. Simon
Rosebridge, Gaspe, P.Q.
Family Herald and Weekly Star
August 18, 1915

Trip Up the Klondyke

Dear Ex-Leaves:

This is my first letter to your corner, but I wrote to the club about two years ago. I became an Ex-Leaf last December.

I will tell you of a trip I took with my husband. We left Dawson in December, there were three of us, my husband and another man and myself. We each had our own dog teams consisting of three dogs.

We travelled nearly two hundred miles up a river named Klondyke to a place called Moose Creek. There we camped,—and put out a few traps, but as we were only amateurs we didn't catch much.

The scenery was grand. I took seventy pictures. I mushed my dogs in 62 degrees below zero and slept in a tent 70 degrees below. One night I slept out in about 58 weather without a tent, right on the snow.

We had several experiences. I wore overalls all the time,—they are the only thing in the woods for they keep you warm and are not so much in the way as skirts.

I am cooking now in a Road House one hundred miles from Dawson. I am sixty-two miles from my nearest lady neighbour.

I will close now, wishing the Club and all its members the best of success.

Musher

Yukon
Family Herald and Weekly Star
October 26, 1916
I hope you will tell us some more of your experiences in the Northwest.—Editor.

Stenography And Typewriting

Dear Maple Leaves:

I am going to say "farewell" to the dear old club. I am past the age limit, but if the Editor will be good enough to print my last letter I shall be much obliged.

I wonder what most of the Leaves think of the club? Do they use it to gain correspondents, or merely for the pleasure of seeing their letters printed in such a famous and widely-read paper as the Family Herald. If so, that is a selfish motive, isn't it? What do you think of it, Editor? Surely this is not so; our club is far too interesting for that. All the letters printed are brimful of interest,—just as if the writers meant what they wrote.

How many Leaves have studied stenography and typewriting? I have. Shorthand is pretty complicated stuff, and typewriting requires very much patience,—a quality difficult to acquire.

At present I am living on a farm eight miles from Port Hope, a large town fronting Lake Ontario. I finished my business courses last June, and am now trying to get a position in an office. Are any of the Leaves in a similar state?

I would like to ask a question, Editor. How can I correspond with Ex-members? Will I send the letter to you, and will you forward them to the Ex-friends?

Dropping Leaf

Clifford Phillips
Port Hope, Ont.
Family Herald and Weekly Star
January 5, 1916

I think my Leaves write to the club for the pleasure it gives them to belong,—also for the enjoyment of correspondence with other members. Doubtless, they are pleased to see their letters in print, but I do not consider this is selfish. The first letter you write to any Ex-member should be sent here in my care, with the pen-name of correspondent on the envelope.—Editor.

Time Keeper on the Railway

Dear Maple Leaves:

I am fifteen years of age and live in Ontario. I have been on the railroad since the sixth of May. I am timekeeper for my father. I think it is the best job I have had yet.

I like to be at home with my brothers and sisters. I wasn't home for six weeks, and I was very glad to see them again.

I like outdoors sports, but cannot take much part in them as I have a stiff leg. I got shot in the knee about a year ago. I was in hospital at Toronto for ninety-one days, and never saw anyone from my home all that time.

I would like to correspond with boys and girls my own age, or anyone that would like to write.

Railroad Bill

William Bridge
North Bay, Ont.
Family Herald and Weekly Star
September 6, 1916

Renews Acquaintance with the Leaves

Dear Maple Leaves:

Since I last wrote I have left home and taken a position with the Reid Newfoundland Co. as night operator. At present I am at Norris Arm, but when a fellow is railroading he does not know when he is going to be shifted. I have been feeling a wee bit homesick, but I guess I'll get over it.

I have seen the Family Herald only once in a month and when I got it, of course, the first thing I look for is the Maple Leaf Club. After reading a few letters I was seized with the desire to renew acquaintance with you.

I think it is the duty of all loyal subjects to do their bit for King and Country, but unfortunately everyone does not seem to realize the duty he or she owes to the great British Empire and the privileges which they enjoy by living under the Union Jack. Newfoundland has sent, and is still sending her bravest sons, and they have won a name for themselves. The Canadians have proved to be as good as any fighters of the Empire, and the Australians and New Zealanders stand by no means in the background. I have one cousin in the Royal Canadian Regiment, and he has come through so far, unscathed.

            Sycamore

H.L. Prince
c/o R. N. Co., Norris Arm, Nfld.
Family Herald and Weekly Star
January 10, 1917

Using the Dictaphone

Dear Maple Leaves:

I am a stenographer in one of the biggest factories in Orillia, but I do more than typewriting and shorthand as I use the dictaphone most of the time.

The Governor General of Canada and his family visited our town on the 19th of June and there was a reception held in the park.

I would like correspondents of my own age (14) or older, either boys or girls. If "Elvira" sees this will she please write.

O.I.C. Kid

Mabel Sears
Orillia, Ont.
Family Herald and Weekly Star
August 28, 1918

Other Books in the Life Writing Series Published by Wilfrid Laurier University Press

Haven't Any News: Ruby's Letters from the Fifties
Edited by Edna Staebler
with an Afterword by Marlene Kadar
1995 / x + 165 pp. / ISBN 0-88920-248-6

"I Want to Join Your Club": Letters from Rural Children, 1900-1920
Edited by Norah L. Lewis
with a Preface by Neil Sutherland
1996 / xii + 250 pp. (30 b&w photos) / ISBN 0-88920-260-5

And Peace Never Came
Elisabeth M. Raab
with a Foreword by Marlene Kadar
1996 / xvi + 183 pp. est. (12 b&w photos, map) / ISBN 0-88920-281-8